PRAISE FOR CAR PARK LIFE

'A retail park *Heart of Darkness*.'
— John Grindrod, author of *Outskirts*

'Compelling, insightful and teeming with mid-life spirit.'
— Andrew Kötting, director of *Gallivant*

'There's no shortage of books nowadays seeking out the hidden corners of our towns and cities, but few set themselves the challenge of exploring seemingly such unpromising terrain as *Car Park Life*. Against the odds, Gareth Rees succeeds brilliantly in illuminating these neglected spaces and in bringing their unexpected stories to life.'
— Merlin Coverley, author of *The Art of Wandering*

'Extraordinary. I loved it, and will never take my Asda car park for granted again.'
— Angela Barnes, BBC Radio 4's *The News Quiz*

'Drives all over the psychogeography genre, and leaves the bodies buried beneath the tarmac.'
— Owen Booth, author of *What We're Teaching Our Sons*

'Knocks "psychogeography" into the dustbin of history where it belongs!'
— Wayne Holloway, author of *Bindlestiff*

D1392410

Also available from
Gareth E. Rees and Influx Press:

Marshland
The Stone Tide

CAR
PARK
LIFE

Gareth E. Rees

Influx Press
London

Published by Influx Press
The Greenhouse
49 Green Lanes, London, N16 9BU
www.influxpress.com / @InfluxPress
All rights reserved.
© Gareth E. Rees, 2019

First edition 2019.
Printed and bound in Great Britain by Clays Ltd, Elcograf S.p.A.

Paperback ISBN: 9781910312353
Ebook ISBN: 9781910312360

Editor: Gary Budden
Copyeditor: Momus Editorial
Cover design: Austin Burke
Cover photograph: Jeff Pitcher
Interior design: Vince Haig

For Simon, co-pilot during the Makro years.

AUTHOR'S NOTE

The book is based on a series of retail car park explorations undertaken between 2015 and 2018. Some of the car parks have since been redeveloped or rebranded, but their essential spirit, or lack of it, lives on. This is by no means a comprehensive collection of British retail car parks, nor is it a complete catalogue of car park experiences. I have only scratched the surface. Everyone has a car park story and I'm sure you have your own. So consider this book a primer. A catalyst. A starting point. Then go out and explore.

Part One
Entry

Chapter One

The Access Road

It is Morrisons in Hastings that lights the fire of my obsession. Not the supermarket itself but the space outside: *the car park*. The attraction is not instant. We don't click immediately. At first, I use Morrisons for the weekly shop, making me just like all the others who traipse between the superstore and the car, laden with bags or pushing a trolley, oblivious to the car park's charms, its mystery, its threat. After a few months, I use Morrisons not only to shop, but also as a shortcut into town. Its car park lies at the other side of an underpass at the end of my road, between a railway embankment and a Victorian street of shops and eateries at the foot of West Hill, a steep elevation behind the Norman castle. I pass through it daily on my way to ostensibly more interesting destinations: the working fishing beach, the pubs, the chippies, the bric-a-brac shops.

One night, I return from the pub and take my usual shortcut through the Morrisons car park. But rather than head directly to my road, I take a look around. I am in no rush and there's something alluring about the car park tonight, caught in bright moonlight after rain. Hooded lamps, crested with gull-deterring needles, shower light onto the tarmac. The yellow glow of the Morrisons sign, reflected in a puddle, has all the sad beauty of a late-night amusement arcade. I slap my foot in the water and see the stars wobble. 'Moondance' by Van Morrison kicks off in my brain. The night's magic seems to whisper and hush as a herring gull boomerangs over the architraves and the ghost of a cleaner flits through the dimly lit interior. Vehicles are scattered here and there. A superstore car park is rarely empty, and never silent. Water trickles from the guttering. A generator hums. There is a squeak of trolley wheels and the rattle of something moving on metallic rails. A slam and bang. Bakers, perhaps, preparing the morning's batch. The disembodied voices of the night shift drift across the lots as I wander in transgressive loops, crossing white lines, disabled parking bays and the petrol forecourt, where I send a startled fox crashing into the hedge. This seems a different, wilder car park to the one in the daytime.

There are others here. By the wall, two boys with skateboards smoke joints beneath a NO SKATEBOARDING sign as a huddle of girls pass around a can of Monster energy drink. A dented sports car rumbles down the access road, driver in a baseball cap, eyes lit up like a cat's in the lamp glare before he veers off into the shadowy perimeter for a reason I cannot fathom, nor dare to discover. Three lanky Polish lads by the entrance talk in low voices and shoot me a dirty look as I veer towards the recycling bins at the perimeter, where a bed frame lies in the shrubs. I pass a Mercedes with a crumpled bonnet and, disconcertingly, a licence plate that includes the number 1066. As I turn back to the supermarket I approach a car with a solitary woman inside. She fumbles with her keys in panic. I pretend to look at my phone so that she knows I have no interest in what she's up to. When I take a glance back she is twisted around in her seat, staring at me, wide-eyed. We remain connected for a torturous moment before she fires up the engine and pulls away. I get a strange sense that I have stumbled onto a drama that connects the woman in the car, the lingering Polish men, the stoned skateboarders and the crashed Mercedes; secret lives that hide in plain sight.

At the rear hedgerow of the car park I notice a sign, which reads:

**THIS DEVELOPMENT IS NOT DEDICATED AS A
PUBLIC RIGHT OF WAY
ENTRY IS ONLY PERMITTED TO SHOPPERS
AND THOSE WITH THE WRITTEN PERMISSION
OF Wm MORRISON SUPERMARKETS PLC
PROCEEDINGS WILL BE TAKEN AGAINST
THOSE ENTERING ONTO THIS DEVELOPMENT
FOR ANY OTHER PURPOSE**

It strikes me that I have entered the car park without any intention to shop, an illegal act in the eyes of the supermarket. The public are not permitted to walk or linger or play here. Proceedings might be taken against them. It feels like a challenge. Car parks are not only places for cars but also thoroughfares for pedestrians. Hangouts for teenagers. They're places to rendezvous. Bump into neighbours. Exchange goods. Get some cash out. Have an argument with your partner. Make an awkward phone call. Eat a quiet lunch away from your colleagues. Secretly munch into a diet-busting burger from that chain you tell everyone you hate. Car parks are an intrinsic part of the landscape, like them or not, and if they are going to encroach on the space where our common grounds, marketplaces, municipal buildings, factories and marshlands once were, then we have a right to interrogate the space, find a way to embrace it, even learn from it. What do we even know about these places? Are they simply slabs of tarmac or are they something more? Do they have the potential to contribute something of worth to society? Or are they pernicious entities, Trojan horses of neo-liberalism, ruining us from the inside? Sites of psychosis, decay and disaster? Someone needs to find out, and this kind of landscape is right up my street. In the same way that a rambler who walks the same route regularly through private land can convert it to a public right of way, given enough time, perhaps I can do this with retail chain store car parks, and help reclaim the space for the good of all.

This is the moment when the *car park nonsense*, as friends and family describe it, takes over my life. I don't know yet how many hours I will lose to car parks, how many cheeky car park diversions I'll take on the way to someplace else. I don't know yet that talking incessantly about car parks and arranging a week-long holiday around a series of car park visits between Hastings and the Scottish Highlands will contribute to the end of my marriage, but I cannot change that future. When the iceberg broke away and the *Titanic* set sail, the two had already converged. In this Morrisons at night, time and space conjoin, and the car-park-me is born. As I savour the thrill of a landscape mutating in significance before my eyes, I realise that a car park can have as much mystery and magic as a mountain, meadow or lakeside. When we hurry through them with groceries on our mind they may look indistinguishable, but like a second-hand book where the previous owner has scrawled notes in the margins, they are full of intriguing human detail. Examine them closely and they come to life. This challenges an assumed truth, that car parks are non-places without geography, nature, social history or cultural nuance. Here, beneath the Norman castle, circled by gulls, with the 1066 Mercedes and the bored teenagers, I feel that I couldn't be anywhere else, and that here is not only a Morrisons, but a multiplicity of places reaching back through time.

In the eleventh century, when Hastings was a Cinque port, this spot would have been at the marshy edge of a bay that give shelter to ships. After cataclysmic storms in the thirteenth century, half the castle collapsed into the bay and caused it to silt up, ending Hastings' role as a locus of sea power. Things took a turn during the late eighteenth-century bathing craze when it became a hotspot for rich folk seeking recuperative waters and salty air. The location of this Morrisons car park became the site of a waterworks and the Hastings & St Leonard's Gas Company. The buildings that fronted Queens Road were known locally as 'the Gas Showrooms' and included an arched entrance into the works, inscribed with the words: *Our Motto is Service*. As the population grew and gas consumption soared, the site became too small. When the council demanded a £4,000 coal levy, the company's shareholders voted to move the works to Bexhill. Only the Gas Showrooms remained, a series of red-brick buildings with a tower that jostled for supremacy with the neo-Gothic steeple of St Andrew's Church next door, the interior of which was decorated by local tradesman Robert Tressell, who would write

The Ragged-Trousered Philanthropists, a novel about the plight of working-class people in a fictional version of Hastings. His book describes the shady dealings of the gas company owners who moved the works to line their own pockets, which gives this car park location a cameo role in the town's radical history.

When the gasometers and tower were levelled in the 1970s, a supermarket was established. On the site of the Victorian church, they built a petrol station in the service of our oil gods. The location of the arched entrance to the Gas Showrooms became the access road to the superstore. On occasions when I walk the dog up West Hill and look down at Morrisons, nestled in the valley by the railway line, I see the ghostly outline of its past: the roofs of amassed vehicles glistening like water in the former marshland; the clock tower on the superstore roof counting the hours until home time for the gas workers; shoppers solemnly filing into the entrance by the petrol station like Victorian worshippers on a Sunday; cars trailing down Waterworks Road ready to stock up for the week; the corporation still trying to impress upon the locals its benevolent intentions. *Our Motto is Service… Morrisons Makes It*. This Morrisons has retained its genius loci as a place of energy, power and influence. It feeds the town with nourishment and fuel; it brings people together. Along the front of the store, benches are placed next to ashtray bins, rows of smokers gazing at car park life going by. There is the sound of chatter. Teenagers laughing. Parents telling their kids off. A sulking dog, tethered to the wall. An elderly couple eating Scotch eggs while waiting for their taxi. The trolley collector clattering past with his precarious train of steel. There are maps of Hastings, Bexhill and Battle on the wall. Taxi numbers and ads for local businesses. You don't get as much sense of community in the car park of a Lidl or an Aldi. The new wave of budget car parks doesn't encourage dwelling. There's nowhere to sit. No advertising. No bins for cigarette ash. No car park attendants. These newcomers dispense of such wasteful fripperies. It makes me sad. Perhaps one day I will look back on my life and remember the car parks of Morrisons with a strange, sentimental yearning.

Chapter Two
Outer Space

Morrisons was not my first car park. It was the catalyst for an explosion, the combustible components of which were forged in my formative years. I believe we all have a childhood retail car park buried deep in our psyche. If we think back to the times we went shopping with parents, took shortcuts through town or sought out territories for illicit teenage activities, most of us could dig up a story that tells us something about the adults we became. Everyone I speak to has a car park of note. It is not always uppermost in their minds, of course. Sometimes it takes cajoling on my part, or a few alcoholic drinks, for the story to come out like a burp, surprising and ugly, yet oddly familiar, a sulphurous whiff of the deep past.

My significant first was the Makro car park in Manchester. My family lived in Glossop, a market town in the Peak District, a mile and a half away from where *The League of Gentlemen* was filmed. On Saturday mornings, my brother and I were ushered into the Mazda, clutching *Star Wars* figures, books or furry puppets, then off we'd go. I'd stare out of the car window at the topography roll by in a blur, the mills of Hadfield, the Victorian bridges of Dinting Vale, and majestic pylons ranged along the busy carriageways, while Dave Lee Travis played the hits of the year: 'Karma Chameleon', 'Billie Jean', 'Club Tropicana', 'Uptown Girl'. Mostly, we would go to the Arndale Centre in the city, but sometimes Mum and Dad craved bulk-buy wholesale bargains, which meant a trip to the Dutch trade 'cash-n-carry' chain store Makro, the Manchester branch of which was on a ring road in the Eccles area. Its interior was forbidden to children under twelve, so my parents would leave me and my brother in the car and vanish through the sliding doors. *What was inside that place?* I envisioned towers of boxes, men in brown coats with clipboards and forklift trucks moving at speed with heavy stacks. A place where no child could survive more than five minutes without being crushed to death, which is why we were banished to the car park.

My brother Simon was eight and I was ten, but we moonlighted as pilots of the Mazda interstellar spaceship – me the captain and Simon a highly expendable crew member. As soon as our parents were out of sight, it was time for action. We leapt into the front seats and buckled up, for belt buckles were a novelty item and there was a thrill to putting them on. In the early eighties, safety was for adults in the front seats. Kids rattled in the back without restraint and smashed like eggs in the event of a crash. It never did me any harm. We never crashed and, if we had, I'd be dead and someone else – or perhaps nobody at all – would be writing a book about car parks. Back then, people didn't know enough about the many ways to die to care about seat belts, or leaving their kids unsupervised, or shutting them in the car while they shopped for low-fat yogurt, light bulbs and muesli at wholesale stores. Simon and I were blissfully ignorant of phantom rapists in the car park who wanted to snatch us for their torture basements. We were concerned only about being at the controls of an intergalactic Mazda with tractor beams and asteroid fields to deal with. I gripped the steering wheel and punched buttons on the cassette player as Simon checked to see if Mum had left anything edible in the glove compartment. The game continued until we grew bored and took things up a notch. I realised that if I opened the door and stood on the passenger seat with my head over the roof, I could view the car park, a galaxy of colourful metallic stars glistering as far as the eye could see. It was time to leave the confines of the spaceship. I jumped onto the tarmac and sneaked around the back of the car, poking my head up at the windows to startle Simon. But he was one step ahead, pulling the passenger door shut and pushing down the locks. Now I was trapped outside.

'Open it!' I tugged at the door.

He laughed, but eventually let me in. That adventure was the beginning of a series of spacewalks. My brother and I took it in turns to exit, circle and re-enter the Mazda, messing with the locks, opening and closing the doors, trapping each other out, until we were both outside the ship with all the locks down and – suddenly – we were locked out of the car. Lost in space. Or not *lost*, but disconnected, severed from the mother ship, exposed to the elements, two fleshy humanoids in a landscape of tarmac and metal. There was no obvious path, no trees, no signs, no escape but through a vale of cars between us and Makro, a menacing grey building in which we were not welcome.

Above us, encroaching cloud blocked out the sun. The air carried voices. The steps of adults approached. Keys rattled. An ignition system shuddered. The whine of a reversing vehicle made us jump. We were too short to see what was going on beyond the few cars around us. The car park had become a hostile world of strangers in unpredictable machines and, worse, Dad was going to be really cross when he came back. It was hopeless. For a while we stood with our palms pressed against the glass, looking in at our *Star Wars* figures. Then we made two plans. One was that we remained here until Mum and Dad returned, which could be hours, days even, perhaps never, leaving us to eke out an existence among the killing machines, drinking rainwater from puddles. The other was that we made our way through the alien car-scape and asked a member of staff to call our parents on one of those tannoy machines. Public humiliation for both them and us. Neither plan was attractive. We tossed the options back and forth until we heard more footsteps, the *clank* and *thunk* of a trolley, and there were Mum and Dad, gods from the heavens come to rescue us.

The gods were angry but merciful, because one of the windows was rolled down enough to get a coat hanger inside and flip the lock, a coat hanger which the child-sceptic overlords of Makro were happy to provide for free.

I stand in the same car park over thirty years later. My imagination might have filled in a few blanks in the story, but then again, the Makro car park of 1983 was always a half-imagined place. I was a ten-year-old boy exploring outer space with his sibling, only to find a strange tarmac world that human adults had created solely for bulk-buy shopping beside monolithic tower blocks and busy carriageways.

Car Park Life

There are many landscapes I remember from my youth – playing fields, reservoirs and cobbled market towns; Derbyshire fells, Kentish cliffs and Spanish beaches – but this car park is as important as any of those places. If anything, it is more influential on the way I see the world. The territories that excite me are the overlooked, mundane places in which I find myself far more often than bucolic idylls. Scrapyards, alleyways, canals, railway sidings, service stations and shopping centres fuel my imagination.

This is why I have come to this car park, a place I haven't visited since my family moved away from Glossop in 1989. I've not thought much about Makro until my interest in car parks began, a fascination that is not shared by my wife and kids who stare at me bleakly from our Peugeot as I prowl with my camera, sniffing the air for a memory. For me, this is an important piece of my history – the origin car park – but I am convinced I've come to the wrong place. This can't be the Makro from my childhood. I found the location on Google Maps and it seems right, geographically, but this car park is smaller than I remember, a puny square of white lines. It's almost empty, although I realise that this is a Tuesday afternoon and as kids we'd have come here on a Saturday. Still, this isn't it. Outside the perimeter there are fields and a scrubland piled with mounds of earth, with diggers rumbling over them. It's as if this Makro is the first in a series of encroachments onto farmland at the edge of the city. I cannot recall the car park backing onto a wilderness. Nevertheless, we are here now and the girls need a wee, so we shamble to the entrance where I'm asked for my membership card. I don't have one. Yet again, I am forbidden to enter Makro. I explain to the woman at the desk – name tag: *Maria* – that my daughters are desperate for the toilet and she directs them through a nearby door. While I wait, I ask her where the original Makro was located, the one from the 1980s.

'This is the same old Makro,' Maria says, laughing. 'I should know because I've worked here since 1979.'

I am overjoyed. While Simon and I were on our car park space adventure, Maria had been right here, inside the building. I feel like hugging her. When Emily and the kids emerge from the toilet I tell them that this is it – *the same Makro* that their dad came to when he was their age. They show absolutely no interest. I explain to Maria why I have come to Makro, not to see the store, only the car park. She shows no interest either, only a flicker of pity.

'I'm thirsty,' says my eldest. Maria kindly offers them some hot chocolate and, despite our lack of Makro cards, leads us towards a cafe. This sparks another mental disruption because I remember being allowed into the cafe at the age of twelve, but it was upstairs, with windows that looked onto the warehouse so you could watch the forklifts.

'There's no public cafe now', explains Maria, 'this is just the staff canteen.'

We pour hot chocolate into plastic cups from the dispensing machine and, thanking Maria, leave as quickly as possible. The girls return to the car with their drinks while I explore. The one aspect of Makro's car park that matches my childhood recollection is the lack of foliage. No islands with trees or shrubby dividers. No pedestrian paths. No child-and-parent parking. The tarmac is marked with plain white lines for cars, yellow bays for the trolleys and gullies for water run-off. Minimalism is key. This place is about trade. Business-to-business. No fripperies. Get in, get out.

Car Park Life

Things become more interesting when I walk down the side of the building into a garden with picnic benches and ornaments. This is a surprise. The nether regions of a car park are usually scruffier zones, out of sight and out of mind. I assume it's an alluring front for the Makro garden section. A path leads into another car park at the rear, marked 'store technician parking'. These are the places you don't imagine exist behind the stores. And why should you? What kind of mind imagines store technician parking?

I return to the main car park via a grassy verge lined with plastic hatches, entrances to subterranean recycling containers, perhaps, or the burial chambers of deceased Makro managers. I hear bird trills as the hedge falls away to reveal a field where a man sits in a tractor, engine turned off, crows circling. The car park is separated from it by a wire fence under attack, its buckled concrete posts consumed by nettles, briars and buddleia, a vision which would have unsettled me as a nine-year-old, the marauding plant from *The Day of the Triffids* being my second most feared monster after the shark from *Jaws*. But I never came to this perimeter. I never knew it was here.

At the far corner I can see the freshly churned land where diggers growl among red pile drivers and men in hard hats yell across flooded pits, beckoning trucks to come tip their stones. *What are they building out there?* I turn to see my kids staring as I photograph the decayed yellow paint of the decommissioned assembly point sign, aware of myself suddenly, and how ridiculous I am. I remember me and Simon in our Mazda spaceship as Mum and Dad moseyed around Makro, hunting for cheap toilet roll. Now my girls watch me explore paint markings outside the store. Is what I am doing any better? Any worse? Any different? I feel a cycle turn. Two eras overlaid. Time dissolving. I marvel at how this place could be so different to how I remember it, and yet be virtually unchanged since I was last here. I get an unsettling feeling that this car park and its environs are nothing more than a chronologically retarded synaptic memory circuit in my brain, and that when I drive away in five minutes' time, everything will stop again until I next return.

Chapter Three
Planet of the Dinosaurs

A few weeks after my inaugural walk around Morrisons I test my proposition on another local superstore car park. I want to check that it wasn't a fluke, a peculiar confluence of events or a fleeting insight that will never recur. I am prone to flights of fancy. Seized momentarily by fantastical visions. An epilepsy of the imagination. It comes and goes, with supreme highs and crashing lows. What seems beautiful in the throes of passion can become ugly the morning after.

> We had a wild night together
> beneath the moon, my dear Morrisons
> but now I wake up with a pounding head
> and a dreadful sense of regret
> before I turn my head
> to see what you really look like.

In the sober light of day, outside another supermarket, I might realise that car parks are just car parks – flat, identikit, devoid of idiosyncrasies – and that there's desperation in my desire to find meaning in them. Perhaps I am yearning for something to convince me that when Britain becomes a flyblown Poundland, its public institutions sold off, its green spaces polluted, its wildlife decimated, there will be moments of magic in what remains of the landscape, some consolation for what we have lost.

It is with immense trepidation, then, that I take the twisting road from my house to Silverhill, a former hilltop farm that became a Victorian turnpike. It remains a busy crossroads between the A21 and Battle Road as they meet on the descent to St Leonards-on-Sea. Queues of cars and buses rumble past a florist, cafe, fried chicken takeaway and post office. Silverhill was the site of the Marshall-Tufflex plastics factory until Asda bought the land in 2007 and built a store on it. 'Mixed regeneration', they called it, promising additional retail units, pedestrian links and a car park in a place notoriously bad for off-road parking. I've been here a few times to shop but paid little attention. I try to picture what I remember from my previous shopping trips. All I see is an amalgam of the other Asdas in my life. Green signs, white markings, trolley bays, cars and zebra crossings. I try to think what else there could be. What if there *is* nothing else, and I don't find anything of note? Then again, what defines something *of note*? Surely a thing which is noted is *of note* by the very act of it being noted. *I note therefore it is*. If all else fails, I can will significance into being. Animate that life which lies dormant in the tarmac.

Burdened with these worries, I cross at the lights onto the concourse of Asda, a wide sweep of tessellated paving slabs beneath the steel-and-glass frontage of the superstore. Immediately, I'm surprised. Some of the slabs are marked by dinosaur footprints. A woman in a blue tracksuit, riding a matching blue mobility scooter, rumbles over the prints, unperturbed. The concourse is separated from the pavement by crude blocks of sandstone to create a prehistoric effect. A raised verge, bordered with similarly misshapen hunks of stone, bristles with a verdant jungle of ferns, fronds waggling in the breeze. Behind is a mosaic frieze depicting colourful dinosaurs, designed by children for a 'Community Inclusion Project'. The dinosaur footprints lead me past the cafe to the main doors, then up to the trolley stacks, where the prints have been painted official Asda green. A sign in a faux-antiquated font says *Welcome to Silverhill Village,* with an array of cartoon dinosaurs above an illustrated map of its roads, with a list of local amenities. There's a green Asda insignia at the bottom. This is history in association with Asda, appropriating the palaeontological legacy of the area.

St Leonards was built by the Victorians as a health resort next to Hastings, which was considered too dirty and disreputable for the upper classes. During construction, extensive quarrying yielded many fossils. Local guidebook writer William Diplock wrote in 1864[1]: 'Remains of Saurians have been found in the neighbourhood of Hastings. The skeleton of a gigantic Iguanodon was discovered in digging the foundation for the new house at Tivoli, called Silverlands.' The Iguanodon was a herbivore which, in my childhood dinosaur books, was usually getting savaged by an Allosaurus, so I was never a fan, but you get the dinosaurs you deserve and the Iguanodon is a very British beast: a duck-faced victim with a herd mentality and spiky thumbs aloft, like Paul McCartney's, to give the illusion that everything is fine.

In 1891, an almost complete Iguanodon was excavated on Silverlands Road, then another on Bohemia Road. Incidentally, specimens from three Iguanodon species

---

1   W. Diplock, *Hastings, Past And Present : With Notices Of The Most Remarkable Places In The Neighbourhood And An Appendix Containing A List Of Books Relating To The District And Other Supplementary Matter,* 1864, p. 341

were discovered by local amateur palaeontologist, Charles Dawson. They were the few genuine finds in a career which became notorious for his archaeological hoaxes, culminating in the discovery of Piltdown Man. For thirty years, these skull fragments were considered 'the missing link', until scientists proved the fragments were aged artificially and placed in ancient alluvial deposits along with manipulated orangutan jaw fragments. After I discover this piece of history, Charles Dawson becomes a character in my autobiographical novel *The Stone Tide*, in which I mock him for his desperate fabrications while hypocritically making up stories about him. The book describes the breakup of my marriage, caused – in part, I am sure – by my obsession with car parks inspired by this encounter with dinosaur history in Silverhill's Asda, in which Dawson played a key role. Revenge is his, it seems. When you start to write about the connections between people and landscape, the synchronicities keep coming. One story begets another story begets another story. Once that wheel gets rolling, it cannot be stopped.

Standing on a dinosaur footprint by the trolley stack, I realise that my Morrisons car park walk was not uniquely unusual. Here is a supermarket car park that has gone full Flintstones, with comedy rocks piled near the entrance among pine trees and spiky yuccas. This aesthetic has caused strain for Asda's health and safety officer. A sign reads: *No climbing on the rocks: Asda will not accept liability for any accidents, damage or injuries incurred*. Yes, this is a hub for tasty foodstuffs, but it is also a wild place where death shows no mercy to the curious.

In this Cretaceous context, the supermarket transforms. The roof has been covered with a net, like an atrium for pterodactyls. The external supports, branched in shape, are a row of majestic redwoods. Below them, an apeman squats by piles of logs and plants, intently smoking. Nearby is the Click & Collect 'drive thru', with its primitive spelling of the word 'through'.

'CAVMAN LUV DRIVE THRU –
– MAYK LYF EEZEE!'

Deeper into the car park, a few of the weaker trolleys have become separated from the herd. In a covered bay, one stands alone, as if too frightened to leave, or perhaps plotting a revolution in which it shall free itself from its hellish zoo and subjugate its rulers, chaining shoppers together and pushing them slavishly through these oily wastelands.

The cigarette-strewn path around the far perimeter is lined with wooden gabions filled with rocks. Bindweed curls through the slats, dotted with white flowers and the odd empty can of energy drink. Signs continue to warn of the perils of climbing. But who cares? There are no security guards, not even many customers in these parts. This is a post-human zone where you can do what you like. A slot machine for pumping air into car tyres stands on the corner, two skinny black tubes protruding from its frontage, like a dishevelled 1950s TV robot. Gone is the saurian theme; I have transcended epochs. I thought I was on the Planet of the Dinosaurs but it turns out that this was Earth all along. A steel fence separates me from a trading estate, the sound of drills and tinny radios drifting from the back of Screwfix, punctuated by blokey shouts and cries. I pass an automated fuelling station where a woman stands by her Corsa, watching the price tick up. I feel uncomfortable suddenly. Something has changed. Not only the atmosphere, but my sense of myself and my locomotion through the landscape. There are new implications to my presence in this perimeter area where there's only this woman and her car. The nether regions of a car park do this to you, physically. Make you feel like you're up to no good. That you have no good reason to be there. That you're up to iffy business.

The woman at the petrol pump doesn't seem concerned as I pass by. We don't look at each other. I try to walk like a regular guy on his way back to a car which he has, inexplicably, parked as far from the entrance as possible. Really I'm on my way to the outlying recycling zone, a mini car park with metal bins for clothes, plastics, cardboard and glass. Nearby, a trolley bay has been smashed up, a tipped trolley to one side, entwined with creepers. A path leads from this wreckage through the trading estate and residential tower blocks. A woman and her husband shamble down the path with their three sons. The woman barks incessantly at them – *Stop running! Stop dawdling! Stop moaning! Hurry up! Slow down!* – slapping them round the head with force. It's blatant child abuse, but what does it matter out here? Civilisation is in tatters. Nobody will ever know, or care.

Returning past the filling station, I am relieved to see a peninsula verge filled with spiky green plants. We are back to the Cretaceous style. I follow the elegant curve of its kerb-beach then walk back to where I started, on the wedge of Flintstones rock, yuccas and monkey puzzle trees beneath the Asda entrance sign. I stand on wood chippings among piles of what looks like dinosaur dung. I kneel to touch them. Still warm. Iguanodons have assembled here recently, sniffing the air for the scent of fresh bread, their guts rumbling, before moving slowly towards their feeding ground.

Chapter Four
The Manifesto

My experience in Silverhill convinces me to continue my explorations. If I can find dinosaurs in an Asda car park there must be plenty more stories to uncover. I need to keep travelling. Walking. Looking. In time, I might stumble upon something to trump the 2012 discovery of Richard III beneath a car park in Leicester, a social or historical revelation that will get me an OBE (which I will refuse with a majestic handwritten letter) and a slot on *Desert Island Discs*, something for which I've already created a playlist in case I ever do something popular and worthwhile.

Richard III was big news. His bones were found beneath a faded letter R painted on a council car park. Nobody knew why the R was there, only that it might have denoted a reserved space. Mick Bowers, a property review officer at Leicester council, said: 'It was something of a standing joke before the dig started that R obviously marked the spot as it seemed a strange thing to spray on a car park[2].' Mathew Morris, who found the skeleton, admitted that the R was 'a bit weird' while the lead archaeologist, Richard Buckley, said the coincidence was spooky. I'm not sure that it was a coincidence but an example of urban geomancy, a magical practice in which messages of cosmic significance can be divined from seemingly random markings and juxtapositions, from paint spills and manhole cover patterns to the coded daubing of builders. The R may have been left there by a psychic council worker, a time-travelling archaeologist, or the ghost of King Richard himself, desperate for a proper funeral. You never can tell.

Because this story astounds on so many levels, it's an A-lister in the genre of car park writing. Admittedly, it's not a huge genre, more a niche within a niche. So far it includes a few books about Richard III and a couple of books that aren't about Richard III. One is *Rethinking a Lot* by Eran Ben-Joseph, an American who argues that car parks can – and should – be aesthetically beautiful, ecologically helpful public spaces. In the USA, car parks take up an area of land the size of Puerto Rico, absorbing heat, contributing to global warming, and exacerbating the problems of extreme weather events like flooding with their damaging levels of surface run-off. Instead, they could be designed more like gardens, with green canopies, porous surfaces, hydraulic systems to capture, distribute and recycle rainwater, public art and extracurricular functions as basketball courts, local markets and concert venues.

Another is called *Parking Mad: Car Parks from Heaven… or Hell* by Kevin Beresford of the Roundabouts Appreciation Society, which describes sixty British car parks, ranging from private to NCP multistoreys to superstores, along with glossy colour photos. Beresford was commissioned by AA Insurance to survey the nation's car parks to boost awareness of their many perils. According to the AA website[3], twenty per cent

3   https://www.theaa.com/insurance/news/car-park-accidents.html

of car insurance claims are for accidents in car parks. This doesn't even factor in all the minor prangs left unreported by those who wish to protect their no-claims bonus. This is unsurprising, perhaps, in an environment in constant motion. Exasperated incomers search for a space. Children run out from behind cars. Drivers chomp on snacks as they pull out, stab at their stereos, tap on satnavs, check smartphones, veer towards shoppers pushing trolleys on notoriously unpredictable casters, unaware that a discarded can or a bump in the tarmac could send their load into a spin, leaving them at the mercy of momentum, gravity, fate. Adults in zombie states lumber towards the store with groceries in mind, not the potential of sudden death beneath bone-crushing steel. Eran Ben-Joseph points out in *Rethinking a Lot*, 'Collision avoidance and pedestrian evasion tend to result in an unorchestrated ballet of machines and people.' The terrain is treacherous. Terrible accidents happen.

A driver yattering on a mobile, view obscured by a box of tissues on the dashboard, runs over a two-year-old in Wembley's Asda.

A six-month-old boy and his two-year-old brother are struck by a car in Sainsbury's, Chichester, as they sit inside a shopping trolley.

A Mitsubishi Colt crashes into the wall of a St Albans Waitrose car park.

A BMW is beached on a concrete slab at a B&Q in Dartford. A year earlier, a Mercedes-Benz driver struggled to remove his car from the very same concrete slab.

At a Co-op in Cumbria, a sixty-eight-year-old reverses into a space but hits the accelerator instead of the brake. She rolls backwards at speed into an upturned shopping trolley, which becomes a ramp, flipping the car into the air and onto its roof. She remains trapped upside down for an hour until the fire brigade free her.

A van bursts into flames outside a Haverfordwest Morrisons as the drivers eat breakfast inside the store.

In the Knaphill Sainsbury's, a young mum is sat in her car with her friend and baby daughter. When she turns the ignition, flames shoot from the wheel arches. 'Get out now!' screams a passer-by. They pluck the child from the car moments before it explodes.

In a Co-op in Baildon, North Yorkshire, there's a four-car pile-up as a pensioner's Kia Picanto smashes through a line of parked cars and crunches into the bollards at the entrance.

It was the propensity of accidents to occur in car parks that instigated the commissioning of Beresford's *Parking Mad*. But as he toured car parks from John o'Groats to Land's End he began to appreciate them in aesthetic and cultural ways, turning his book into more of an affectionate travel guide than a health-and-safety critique. Quite clearly, the man is an enthusiast.

When I am told about the existence of *Parking Mad*, I feel like Captain Scott when he first saw the Norwegian flag of Amundsen fluttering over the North Pole. Beaten to it. Beresford has travelled the length of the country cataloguing car parks on behalf of the AA, publishing a comprehensive collection in a hardback cover. He is the *car park guy*. He's been on the radio. So what does that make me? Shakin' Stevens to his Elvis? Tori Amos to his Kate Bush? Oasis to his Beatles? Am I simply retreading trodden ground? Of course, we walk trodden paths for a good reason. They lead somewhere, even if only to a tar pit filled with the bones of our foolish predecessors. Whatever the destination, we each have our own way of experiencing the journey, and no place remains static, nor objective. It's ridiculous to say that there is only room for one book about the Cairngorms, one book about travelling in Peru, one book about wild swimming or one book about car parks. Beresford has his own point of view. I have mine. The petrolhead from Bournemouth who uses Currys for late-night boy-racing has his point of view, as do the two women who meet in a B&Q car park every Saturday to conduct a clandestine lesbian affair, the taxi driver who parks up each day to eat his Sainsbury's prawn sandwich, and the sex pest who likes to flash his bits outside Norwich Morrisons.

Parking Mad brings together pub car parks, municipal car parks, private car parks and multistoreys, but mine is a mission to explore those nebulous places around our chain stores, hotels and restaurants, in which the user is not necessarily cognisant of its boundaries, whether legal, moral or physical, where the order of things is uncertain. Retail car parks are created for the facilitation of purchases within the store, but they are also shortcuts, meeting places, sights of sexuality, violence and boredom, accident hotspots, loci of personal drama and childhood memories. This is what interests me. There is an untold story here. However, I must be careful. Writing about place can revitalise perceptions of a lesser-known landscape but it risks cultural appropriation when the explorer becomes a Dr Livingstone sticking his flag in other people's neighbourhoods, as if they have just discovered them. The trend is a familiar one. Film-makers, writers, artists and academics pounce on an overlooked urban area and fetishise its rawness, liminality, decay. They share their work on Instagram, Twitter, Facebook, Tumblr and Wordpress blogs. They move into cheap property or squat in disused buildings. They make music and art. They hold parties. They exert a gravitational pull on others like them. Soon the overlooked place moves into sharp focus, until it is the latest fashionable spot for those wishing to buy into an artistic lifestyle at a budget price, attracting entrepreneurs who wish to sell them coffee, beard oil and vintage furniture. Once developers get a whiff of this they buy up abandoned factories, warehouses and townhouses. The people who already live there must put up with being gawked at by self-styled inner-city astronauts in Converse trainers until they get priced out of the area by skyrocketing property values, while their shops and pubs are taken over by the Farrow-and-Ball brigade, with their quail egg bar snacks and beer that tastes of grapefruit.

It's a danger for me. In my final week in East London, as my book *Marshland* went to print, I took a walk with my dog, Hendrix, through Hackney and Walthamstow Marshes, the places I had been writing about for the past three years. The sun glinted on electricity pylons as I crossed a field from a defunct Victorian aqueduct towards the Lee Navigation. A stocky man in his fifties approached, a collie padding ahead of him.

'Watch out for her!' he said, pointing at his dog. 'She's on heat.'

'Oh, don't worry,' I said pointing at my own dog, 'he's been done.'

The man shook his head angrily. As he passed me, he turned and blurted: 'Why the hell would you want to do that? Why would anyone do that to a dog? You've taken his manhood!'

Truth was, my dog was castrated because he was born with defective eyes and it was unethical to let him breed. Furthermore, this stranger was anthropomorphising my dog with the term *manhood*, suggesting that this was really about his own insecurities. But ultimately, it was none of his business.

'It's none of your business,' I said.

His face flushed red. 'You… you…. you… you and your lot have ruined Hackney, totally RUINED IT!' The spittle of his wrath caught the sunlight. 'Because of you fuckers I have to move away. You ponce! Newbie!'

Instinctively, but somewhat unwisely, I raised my middle finger. He bowed his head, shoulders around his ears, trembling like a bull about to charge. I realised there was a good chance I was about to get murdered on the marsh, an appropriate end to my adventures and a potential boon for posthumous book sales.

'Next time I see you,' he yelled, 'I'm gonna give you a Hackney slap!' With that, he strode away. When I got home and googled 'Hackney Slap', I found nothing except the title of a dubstep instrumental. Perhaps it was an ultra-localised term for a punishment beating.

Five years on, I think about this incident and it breaks me out in a sweat. The Hackney Slap is my Sword of Damocles. I may have moved from London but it hovers above me still, forcing me to interrogate myself thusly:

Can I ruin superstore car parks?
And if I did, would it matter?
What's the worst that can happen?

I decide to mull it over with a bottle of wine. It's the only way I can get to grips with something without being trolled by my own neuroses. I decide that the only victims here are the corporations who run the chain stores. International retail giants with power and money. In the unlikely event that I write a book so popular that I encourage an influx into the car parks of our nation, their proprietors will be forced to police their establishments to prevent loiterers infiltrating the space – costing them money, exposing them as corporate fascists and souring their relationship with the public – or they will be forced to make car parks more like *parks*, letting locals linger, explore and play. Skateboards after dark. Basketball hoops. Trees and shrubs that attract wildlife. Can that be a bad thing? But then again, where would teenagers go to smoke joints and drink cans? What would become of the doggers, boy-racers and dealers who also frequent the car park at night? This is the same argument I made against corporate leisure developments in the Lea Valley – that London needed a wild, untamed, shared dream-space. In which case, could this function be ascribed to car parks? If so, it's a sad indictment of our urban landscape that the side of a Tesco could assume the role of a wilderness. But I am determined to find out, even if it results in a Hackney Slap. *To hell with the haters*. I waggle my glass at an imaginary accuser. *I am a car park user, just like anyone else*. I have lived in many locations, from Glasgow to Manchester to Cardiff and Hastings, and when I look back on it, car parks have been a consistent landscape thread, even in my London days when I didn't own a car but walked through the Hackney Tesco or Dalston Sainsbury's, hauling as much frozen food and lager as I could without the handle slicing through my fingers. Car parks don't tend to feature in landscape writing, novels or memoirs, yet a seam of car park experience runs through my life, an alternative version of my history. What will happen if I edit out everything *except* car parks? There is something to be uncovered here, I am sure. But I'm aware that I need to formulate some rules, so I switch on my laptop and sketch out a crude manifesto:

WALK THE TERRAIN. Always walk into the car park, never drive there as a customer. Avoid the psychological mutations that occur at the wheel of a motor. Resist the lure to shop. Transgress the function of the environment as prescribed by corporate architects.

CHAINS ONLY. No private car parks. No stadiums or pubs. No NCPs. No multistoreys. No brutalist porn. Focus on chain businesses like Tesco, Morrisons, Sainsbury's, McDonald's, KFC, Pizza Hut, Harvester, Wicks, B&Q and Currys, Premier Inn and Holiday Inn. These are the less considered spaces. Unplaces. Identikit cookie cutter brandscapes. But don't accept this assumption as truth. Investigate!

NO MOTORWAY SERVICE STATIONS. Service stations are outliers on busy motorways and A-roads. Places of transit, like airports. They're not part of the local urban infrastructure and rarely pedestrian thoroughfares. They're another subject, for another book.

NO INTERVIEWS. Don't interview supermarket managers or architects about what they intend their retail space to be. The official story does not matter. Experience the car park in an empirical way, through your feet, eyes and ears. See the naked lunch at the end of the fork.

ONLY FIVE POINTS IN A MANIFESTO. I can't think of any more rules, but five seems like a good number.

It's a rough draft and needs refinement, but it will do for now. I press PRINT, then Blu-tac it to the wall beside my computer.

'There,' I say, quietly. 'There.'

Tottenham Hale Retail Park

Street trading is
prohibited on
this site

Chapter Five
Dodgy Deals

It comes back to me, that visceral memory of heavy carrier bags slicing into my fingers. Writing my manifesto, thinking back to the car parks of my life, I remember those superstores I frequented in London before a I owned a car, when I could only buy what I could carry, stopping every fifty yards to give my hands a break, swapping the heavier bags to a different arm. I never thought to take a cab, something I considered excessively expensive, despite having no qualms about buying a round of drinks in a pub. That pain in my hands brings back another recollection, too: the Chinese pirate DVD sellers. I've not thought about them in many years, but now they re-emerge, ghostly, from behind the parked cars in my mind, clutching poor copies of *Kill Bill 2*, *The Bourne Supremacy* and *Hellboy*.

In 2004, I lived in a basement flat on a street behind the Hackney Empire, before the Cock Tavern became a craft ale microbrewery, before the Ocean music venue became the Hackney Picturehouse, before the Foxtons estate agents' office cast its shimmering ambience across the fume-choked street. A stone's throw from these was the Tesco superstore on Morning Lane, its car park in the lee of the Silverlink line from Hackney Central to Homerton. The place was always bustling. Shoppers flowed down Narrow Way, a pedestrianised thoroughfare lined with pound shops and greasy spoon cafes, towards a stepped entrance into the car park.

In London, where astronomical rents and property prices swallow up your income, and in which it can take an hour to drive a mile on a busy day, half the population don't own a car; even more in a deprived borough like Hackney in 2004. In my days frequenting the Morning Lane Tesco, this meant there was a high volume of people on foot, moving through a mass of stationary vehicles, towards the exit onto Mare Street. Sellers of pirate DVDs, almost all of whom seemed to be Chinese, formed a human net to catch people moving towards their cars, or towards the exit, fanning out the sleeves to display recent blockbusters and even films that had not yet been released in the UK, poorly recorded, occasionally with a head blocking the view. At the time, the film industry bemoaned the pirate market for killing their profits, little realising that they were wagging their finger at a shark while a massive tidal wave loomed behind them, made up of foaming torrents, DDL links, YouTube, social media and fibre optics. Within a decade, people would share films, music and games for free in the blink of an eye across global networks too numerous to police. But in 2004, when new DVDs cost £15 or more, black market DVD prices were a bargain, and the more copies you bought, the lower the price. The Chinese DVD sellers of the Morning Lane Tesco mastered the art of discreet omnipresence, standing like Gormley statues among cars, lungs presumably blackened by exhaust fumes. They became such an intrinsic feature of the landscape that I would have found their absence strange.

That winter I moved away from that part of Hackney, and the Sainsbury's in Dalston became my local store.

Car Park Life

I returned to the Morning Lane Tesco a few years after, when my wife and I bought a flat in Lower Clapton, but there were no DVD sellers. In 2009, a Walthamstow entrepreneur named Khalid Sheikh and his two sons were convicted of counterfeiting millions of blockbuster movies, exploiting vulnerable Chinese illegal immigrants to do their dirty work[4]. The disappearance of the DVD sellers was probably linked to their arrest, but their time was over anyway. This was already a new era of online piracy, one which did not require vendor foot soldiers to patrol public spaces. Now the only reminder of their existence is the occasional, anachronistic *'Warning: avoid counterfeit DVD sellers'* signs bolted to the walls of supermarkets.

There is a natural inclination for traders to gravitate to superstore car parks. After all, these stores are based on street markets and covered markets. They attempt to fulfil a similar role, offering a variety of products in one place, allowing people the freedom to browse and compare. The founder of Tesco, Jack Cohen, was a market trader who flogged salvaged goods on the streets of London after the First World War, so the DVD sellers of the Hackney branch would not feel so unfamiliar to him. The store's owners might loathe the presence of unsanctioned vendors on their premises, but it is they who have used advertising, branding and architecture to suggest that their businesses are like markets, their stores essential to life (*'Every little helps'*) and their premises intrinsic parts of the urban landscape, whether it's the faux-retro clock towers favoured by Morrisons or the renovated Victorian facades favoured by many in-town Sainsbury's and Tesco.

The more a car park is integrated into a town, the more likely that everyday life takes place in the space. Couples argue. Parents scold children. Teens play-fight. Amidst

4   *The Guardian*, 9 July 2009,   https://www.guardian-series.co.uk/news/4482834.waltham-forest-fake-dvd-gang-convicted

the rattle of trolleys, idling engines and slamming doors, people feel unnoticed, with freedom to act as they might do in the privacy of their homes. The ubiquity of the chain store breeds a familiarity bordering on contempt. They're there to use and abuse. Which means they're often chosen as the location for a shady deal. After all, who notices what's happening between a couple of parked cars outside Tesco? Who pays attention to someone lingering on the perimeter? The British obsession with minding our own business becomes highly concentrated in retail zones, where we focus on what we need to buy, and doing it quickly. Cars come in, cars go out. One may contain a family of four on their weekly shop, the other might contain gangsters with guns. Nobody can tell. Nobody cares. It's the perfect cover.

Of course, the law of averages means that at some point, people get caught.

In 2015, an undercover policeman is outside the Asda in Skelton, waiting for his colleague to emerge. He sees a Mini nearby with a woman and two children inside. A man approaches the car. The window winds down and the man passes a roll of notes into the car. The woman passes three small packages of heroin back to him. A few moments later, she is busted in front of her kids.

That same year, undercover police wait outside a Sainsbury's in Darlington as Mathieu McEvoy enters the car park with a huge batch of amphetamine. He meets George Bell, who hands him £11,840 in cash. Bell is in financial trouble with his drug dealer and carries out the exchange to pay back some of the debt. Alas, the police already know about the deal and arrest both men on the spot.

In 2014, police find a baton on the floor of the Click & Collect area near a van with a smashed window and cannabis worth four grand, the aftermath of a deal gone wrong.

Outside an Iceland, drug dealer Tyrone John stabs one of his customers five times, then flees on his motorbike. Helicopters follow him down the M4 before he exits towards the Westfield shopping centre, where he abandons his car and runs into the mall, evading capture.

At the Co-op in Telford in 2017, police are covertly filming as four men turn up in three vehicles and exchange a holdall containing fifteen kilograms of cocaine.

In 2018, police surround a weed dealer outside the Tesco Express in Charlton. In the same year, two men are busted outside the Asda in Whitchurch with over £3000 worth of cocaine.

The moral of these stories might be that retail car parks are not the best place to buy and sell drugs. Or on the contrary, they show that they are very best place to buy and sell drugs. These busts might consist of 0.00001 per cent of all deals done. For all you know, half the cars in the car park are either full of drugs or full of people wanting to buy drugs.

It's not only drugs that are exchanged in car parks. In 2013, a Lithuanian man drives his Ford Focus into the Gallagher Retail Park in Wednesbury and parks outside Currys. He carries a shopping bag to a parked Mercedes and pops it in the boot. As the Mercedes drives away, a police car tails it and eventually stops the driver, finding three semi-automatic pistols, live ammunition and a latex mask of Frankenstein's monster, the ingredients for an armed robbery.

Even cars are sold in car parks. Two shady Hampshire car dealers named Stan Rudgley and Richard Burbage have a long history of selling defective or untaxed vehicles, refusing to refund customers or fobbing them off with bouncy cheques. When their dealerships are closed down by trading standards, they re-emerge at the Sainsbury's on Fareham Industrial Estate, where they use its car park, shared with Staples and Dreams, as an unofficial forecourt, leaving prices on the windscreens of vehicles. They also set up an online car dealership which they operate from Ophelia's Boutique, a lingerie shop run by Lorraine, Richard Burbage's wife.

In 2015, she and Burbage attend a Sunday afternoon football match. To reward her for enduring the football, Burbage offers to take her out to dinner. Her heart sinks as they pull up outside a KFC. This is not what he promised. Inside the restaurant, they erupt into an argument. As customers grow uncomfortable they are asked to leave. In the car park, their argument escalates until the two are yelling and screaming at each other. At this point, Julian Raffle, a washing machine engineer, arrives on the scene. Raffle is visiting KFC with his family and does not appreciate the effing and jeffing. He approaches the Burbages and tries to calm the situation down, telling them, 'You can't do this here.' This infuriates Burbage, who tries to deck the interloper with two uppercuts. Alas for Burbage, Raffle is a washing machine engineer by day, but a jiu-jitsu expert by night. He deftly blocks the punches and flings Burbage to the ground, where he pins him down until the police arrive.

Raffle later tells the *Southern Daily Echo*: 'He definitely messed with the wrong bloke.' Or, as I like to say these days: 'That's car park life.'

Chapter Six

The Ancestor

In 2400 BC, a young man waves goodbye to his mother and father as he leaves his village in the Alpine mountains and descends to the flatlands, where he follows the Long West River to the Stone Land, trading trinkets from his homeland in return for safe passage through swamps and hostile territories. He charters a vessel across the sea to the Northern Isle, his final destination. Upon reaching shore he spends the night in a cave, his sleep disturbed by howling wolves. The next day, he begins his long march north through a forest towards the great plain where he hopes to make his fortune. He is an expert in metals, able to fashion copper, bronze and gold into tools, weapons and jewellery for the adornment of priests and nobles. Others have made a similar journey, not only metallurgical artisans but makers of ceramic beakers. Word has spread that a talented craftsman can accumulate great power in this crucible of technology, where powerful elites are building temples and seek those with skills and knowledge to join them.

Close to exhaustion, he arrives at the brow of a hill above a basin in the chalk downland, where a river loops and, on a ridge to the east, smoke coils from huts. With a deep breath he walks towards a community of poets, healers and artisans which he will call home for the rest of his life.

True to his reputation, the young man delivers a wondrous knowledge of metals and how they can be manipulated. In demonstrations he shows them how to make bronze axes, head tresses of gold, bracelets and earrings, letting his hands speak as he casts the metal in fire before shaping, sharpening and polishing. He is given a house surrounded by pine palisades an hour's walk from the new temples. Quickly, he picks up the language, rules and etiquette of this society. His friends and neighbours are talented masons charged with crafting the gigantic bluestones left by ancient ice floes, before they are hauled onto the plain and raised into position by hundreds of men using wooden cantilevers. Among them, our hero rises to prominence. A wife bears him three sons and two daughters. Aged thirty-eight, he sustains a serious injury when a support beam snaps and his leg is smashed by falling wood, giving him a permanent limp and infection of the bone. But old age does not bother him, nor does death as it approaches. As a young man he departed his world in the mountains for a new one across the sea, an experience which enriched him, and soon he will enter another realm, satisfied that he has fulfilled his earthly potential. His tools have helped create the ceremonial corridors of wooden pillars, embankments and doorways running from river to temple, where leaders and priests are carried on their final journeys. He has seen his gold adornments on the heads of noblemen. He has ushered in an age of advancement in which humankind can trace the movement of the stars, anchor the heavens to the earth and time their crops to perfection. He has seen divine light blast into the temple at the setting sun of the shortest day and at the rise of the sun on the longest day, at the sight of which he dropped to his knees, opened wide his arms and gave thanks for life's bounty, full of joy that his place in the universe was secure. His deeds will last for an eternity, nourishing generations. If this is what can be achieved now, imagine what the world will be like for those whom would call him their *ancestor*.

It is good. All good. With a smile, he closes his eyes for the last time.

In a well-attended funeral ceremony, they bury him with some of his masterworks to take to the next world. Time passes. His flesh is consumed by bacteria and his barrow is covered by more and more earth until it is indistinguishable from the land around. Above him are laid the bodies of Romans who come to this basin and farm grain, followed by Anglo-Saxons who build their settlements here too. The place in which he lies becomes known as Amesbury, home to an abbey founded by Queen Ælfthryth. He knows nothing about this, nor does he hear the rumble of Norman carts as William the Conqueror's men surge through the land.

Centuries later, the first of the antiquarians study the remains of the stone temple network where he worked, and have no idea what it is. This historical theorising is cut short by civil war as Cavalier occupiers in Amesbury are ousted by Roundheads, who are ousted by Cavaliers again, trampling the earth in pitched battles, hacking each other to pieces. Our noble metallurgist does not stir when a great highway rumbles with stagecoaches from London to Exeter, then engine-powered cars on what is now known as the A303. He doesn't feel tremors as guns boom over Salisbury Plain in preparation for two World Wars, nor hear the Cold War jets scream overhead. A band called The Beatles play their instruments with his stone temple in the background for a moving picture they call *Help!* In the decade that follows, long-haired revellers smoke hashish and trip on acid among the stones. The site is ringed with rope. UNESCO call it a World Heritage Site and scientists come to probe its secrets. In 2002, archaeologists are excavating the site of a new school in Amesbury where there was once a Roman cemetery. Beneath the Roman fragments they discover our hero's skeleton surrounded by a remarkable cache of artefacts: a wristguard, bone pin, copper knife, boar tusk and stash of flints. They say he was one of the specialists who came from Europe's Beaker culture at the dawn of the Bronze Age with advanced metallurgical and ceramic skills. At first they call him the King of Stonehenge, a mighty name, if a little overstated, but later they call him the Amesbury Archer because of the arrowheads buried with him, a humiliating demotion. He was no archer. He was an artisan, innovator and educator. If he hadn't been dragged from his grave and shoved into the museum, he'd be turning in it.

Four thousand, four hundred and twenty years after the metallurgist left his home in the Swiss Alps, I say goodbye to my mother and father and walk out the door with a small bag on my back for the journey ahead. Admittedly, it is not as great a journey as the Amesbury Archer's, for I am already in Amesbury. It's where my parents have lived for the past two decades. My destination is ten minutes up London Road to the Solstice Park, a 160-acre business park a mile away from our ancient hero's resting place, occupied by mega-structures that house Home Bargains, Muller Wiseman and Tintometer. It's a relatively new development, with skeletons of warehouses rising from churned earth. The area closest to the A303 is a zone of chain restaurants called Midsummer Place, offering respite to locals and travellers on the last stop before Stonehenge, including Co-op, Pizza Hut, Costa, KFC and McDonald's. It is also home to a branch of Harvester called The Amesbury Archer in tribute to the great man, selling a range of grilled steaks, burgers and salads, as he would have wished.

The Solstice Park is a place that would have struck the Amesbury Archer with great wonder and confusion. But there is a lot he would recognise from back in his temple days. The road names allude to astronomical phenomena: Solar Way and Equinox Drive and Solstice Road. There are works of manipulated metal: a sculpture of an upturned helicopter called *The Dragonfly* to link the natural world with the military technologies that this landscape hosts. Overlooking the road and the park is a fenced encampment for Bulford Barracks on a camber of green, clustered with pylons, telegraph poles and signal masts. This is a place of control. Of power. As it has always been.

Endless streams of delivery trucks rumble down the access roads as incoming cars cruise towards their desired restaurant. Like Pinocchio, Midsummer Place yearns to transcend its artifice and be a real town. The restaurants are nestled in cul-de-sacs with tree-lined roads. The twenty-four-hour Drive-Thru McDonald's has the veneer of a local pub with its wood-finished seating area, surrounded by retro street lamps and signs for free Wi-Fi. There's even a *Please respect our neighbours and keep the noise down* sign, as you might find outside a pub in a residential area of town, although the neighbours here are Costa and KFC, and the loudest noise is the roaring A303.

In a bay there's a truck with a cylindrical container, the size of a space rocket, which I assume contains something explosive. Dwarfed in its shadow, a man sits happily reading a newspaper, next to a couple smoking dangerously close by. A group of soldiers amble towards KFC as cars queue in the Drive-Thru channel. A woman waiting in her Renault by the kiosk stares with suspicion as I stroll through the drivers-only area on foot, then cross KFC's car park in a reckless diagonal, through wood chippings that separate it from Pizza Hut. As I move between the parking bays of rival franchises I can sense the transition in the variegated corporate colouring, their external lighting like a glue, holding you until you break the spell and are ensnared by the next illumination. However, most visitors don't transcend these boundaries. They drive directly to their preferred franchise, parking as close as they can to the door, then move quickly towards the restaurant. Everyone here knows what they are doing and where they are going. No need for browsing. Everybody knows what each building will provide, right down to the menu details, even before they turn off the ignition. That's the beauty of the chain. It's a universally understood religion.

The more I wander, the more this place feels like a temple, with people going about their rest-stop rituals. Past the Co-op and petrol station I reach the Holiday Inn, the temple's symbolic heart, where 4,000 years fall away. On the lawn, a giant man rests on his knees, hands outstretched to the sky as if in thanks. Sunshine flashes on his scalp. His back and shoulders reflect in the hotel windows, where sales executives eat chicken salads and sip pinot grigio. This is *The Ancestor*, a seven-tonne steel statue erected at Stonehenge in 2010, then moved here to become guardian of the park, this man of metallurgical genius who came from Europe to usher in the Bronze Age. A craftsman who fell to his knees at the sight of the solstice sun glaring through the bluestones. He is an attempt to connect this community of twenty-first-century fast-food franchises with the ancient people, to make a link between sun worship and the Golden Arches, to somehow replace what is lost in the landscape. The forgotten secrets. The buried mysteries. The missing knowledge. The wrong turnings for humankind since he once kneeled here and praised the light.

Chapter Seven

Drake's Leat

My friends Dan and Jane are historians who live in Devon. For many years before the kids come along I visit them regularly for long weekends in their sixteenth-century cob cottage, the walls of which are crumbling to bits, presumably because they are made from mud, straw and sand. Returning from a holiday, they discover water soaking through the ceiling of the living room from a burst pipe. Dan prods at the ceiling with a stick to check the damage. It gives way and he is showered with mummified rats. After this turning point in their love affair with sixteenth-century cob, they move to a house in Tavistock, which they need to knock into shape. To buy DIY materials, they frequent the Crownhill Retail Park in Plymouth, off the Tavistock road, where there is a large B&Q. One day, their inquisitive four-year-old daughter Hester stumbles upon what looks like a dried-up stream running through the car park. Worried that she's about to fall down the bank, Dan bundles her into the car and they head home. No time for another trip to casualty. They've a house to paint. But Dan is intrigued by the mystery feature. He mentions it to me on the phone as we talk about my new-found fascination with retail chain car parks. Dan is researching a book about coaching inns, which will include the first car parks of sorts, albeit for horses and carriages. The difference is that Dan gets paid by a university to go up and down the country looking at inns, while I can only explore retail car parks in the minimal amount of free time I get between work and childcare, which means I have to take opportunities to catch one wherever I travel – on the way to meetings, funerals, weddings and the homes of friends. Dan and I decide that on my next trip to Devon, we will go to the Crownhill Retail Park.

'You might be disappointed,' Dan warns as we approach, months later. He knows that, with me, it's better to keep the bar low. 'It's a regular car park really,' he continues. 'Not much to look at.' I can understand his concern. Dan and Jane have criticised me in the past for not appreciating the scenery fully enough when they drive me through the countryside. The problem has always been that hills don't interest me as much as streets. Trees not as much as pylons. Foliage not as much as litter. It's an issue, I know. I'm not proud. But Dan is wrong to worry about me being disappointed. I've changed. Or rather, I have *been* changed. Ever since my Morrisons night-walks and that journey into the Makro of my childhood, I've been infected with a virulent form of enthusiasm, similar to that which must motivate the trainspotter, in which the reward synapses in my brain go into overdrive when I discover even the tiniest micro-detail of interest – a lost umbrella, a poorly punctuated piece of graffiti, a glimpsed weed deal, a mysterious arrow painted on a drain cover, a man crying in a Vauxhall Astra. I've explored dozens of chain store car parks to test my theory that they're interesting, and I've not yet been disappointed. There's always something to discover. As it turns out, this car park will surpass my expectations. This is the car park that will finally convince me to write a book about car parks.

———————

We drive from Tavistock over the south-west edge of the moor, through patchwork fields on a single-lane road, past a former seventeenth-century coaching inn and the Yelverton golf club, before we hit the dual carriageway into Plymouth. Dan and I agree that it's important not to drive into the retail park itself. If we're to shake off the shopper mentality we must be pedestrians, but not like those pedestrians who seek the safest, most convenient route to the store. We must hike into the car park as if we're about to head up a Scottish Munro or enter an unexplored jungle in the Amazon. In an ideal scenario we'd pitch a tent on the nearest roundabout the night before and dine on roasted rat, poached from the traps behind Pizza Hut. We'd stare up at the night sky, obscured by light pollution, and count the street lamp stars – So many! So beautiful! – followed by a rendition of 'Kumbaya' as we sit around a bonfire of pallets. But instead, we park at neighbouring council offices on a featureless slab with numbered lots denoting who can put their car where, the equivalent of passive-aggressive Post-it notes on milk cartons in the office kitchen fridge that scream *'Not for you!'* We are rebel explorers who don't play by the rules, so we take a spot regardless.

The retail park lies in the lee of Crownhill Fort, built in the 1860s to defend Plymouth from French attack, decommissioned in 1986. Its steep green ramparts loom behind us as we head into the car park via the NO PEDESTRIANS access road between Marks & Spencer and B&Q. Incoming cars force us into pampas grass on the verge. A driver in a pork pie hat stares at us in distaste. His wife looks straight ahead, as if acknowledging us will only encourage our deviant behaviour. Another driver slows down and beckons at us to cross to the footpath, but I don't want to run to safety. I am busy taking photos through pampas grass of some parked trucks that, from this angle, look like elephants drinking at a jungle watering hole. I know the driver hates me for it, almost as much as I hate myself.

Eventually, we're off the road, crossing the bollard-lined pedestrian walkway that traverses the entrance of a monstrously large B&Q frontage. The neatly bricked pedestrian pathway is lined with logs, trolleys, pot plants, bags of compost and special offer signs. The doors hiss and bang at the exit of three men with varying degrees of hair loss. Dan and I keep going until we reach a tall gabion packed with stones that forms the far wall. CAUTION SITE ENTRANCE says a sign on the ground, propped up against an area of gabion that clearly isn't an entrance. Further along there's a weird, yellow, rusted contraption, about shin-high, with no discernible front or back. It's like a trailer except instead of wheels, there are brushes underneath. Perhaps it's a form of car park scrubbing machine to be attached beneath a truck or towed behind a van. Neither of us know. Whatever it is, it's on the verge of collapse. Nearby is a graveyard of rickety old B&Q trolleys, tagged with labels that read SCRAPPED, linked by rusty chains. Within the pile is an anomalous Somerfield trolley. Somerfield hasn't existed as a brand name since 2011, evidence that this trolley limbo zone has existed for more than half a decade. Some of the trolleys have orange plastic flaps that say underneath: IF YOU FIND ME I MAY BE LOST PLEASE PHONE MY OWNER 0845 609 6688. A pathetic plea for help that nobody will hear.

> Give the ALL CAPS a rest, old trolley.
> Nobody is coming for you.
> Nobody cares about you.
> You were pushed around for years.
> But your services are no longer required.
> There is no place for you any more.
> You have been discontinued.
> Banished to the car park fringe.
> Where eventually you will rust and crumble.
> Your bones swept away by the wind.

It's not an easy life out in the B&Q badlands, a lawless place in which feral youth dwell after dark. There are black tyre skid marks from late-night cruising, where petrolheads gather to show off their car modifications or watch each other perform wheelspins, burnouts and doughnuts, high on adrenaline and White Lightning. Discarded scraps of cardboard have been used as makeshift mats, for sitting with friends to watch the spectacle while the moon is high and everyone is happy and young and cold.

While this is fascinating, I'm aware that this car park trip is unique, in the sense that there is a definitive goal in mind. I am seeking a grail: the dried-up stream of which Dan spoke. It is uppermost in our minds, tantalising us with possibilities. This lingering by the decommissioned shopping trolleys is nothing but preamble, and we know it. But perhaps this is the correct order of things, like a romantic dinner date in which a starter must precede a main course must precede dessert must precede inviting the B&Q car park home for coffee, must precede grappling with each other's bits on the sofa. Patience is what we need. Patience. But I'll admit, I can already feel the vinegar strokes.

We circle the perimeter hedge towards Pizza Hut, lined with rat traps, streamers of toilet roll dangling from the foliage. I can't bring myself to sniff or touch to check if they are fresh; I am not Ray Mears. At the fire door, two chairs are angled towards each other, the ghosts of dead gossip in a fag break long gone. The adjacent KFC is closed while its car park is resurfaced. The diggers aren't moving. Men in yellow jackets stare at piles of gravel and check their phones. At the closed Drive-Thru service hatch, the *Pick Up Here* sign points downwards at a wheelie bin that's been moved there to emphasise just how closed it really is, in case anyone stands there waiting for chicken that will never come.

Just beyond the KFC, we come to a dainty wooden footbridge. Beneath it is our much-anticipated destination: a dried-up stream, just as Dan described, lined with pebbles and running in a straight line through the car park, bordered by steep inclines of dry grass, lined with pine trees. We clamber over the railings like naughty kids and drop onto the stones. It is clearly a man-made feature, lined on both sides with stone, outflow hatches indicating that water must once have flowed here. We follow it north towards the B&Q badlands, but as we get closer to the centre of the car park the route is blocked by a grass bank and we're forced up from the channel, where we find ourselves in a circular concrete space, enclosed by a wall. A metallic information sign adorned with text and illustration gives us the answer to the mystery of the stream.

I am gobsmacked. In car park exploration terms, this is the money shot. Dan and I have been walking up a *leat* – an engineered watercourse dating to 1591, built to end the water shortage in Plymouth, a situation so bad that mill owners did not have enough water to power their wheels and so carted the stuff into the town. The Plymouth Corporation decided to construct a waterway to connect the town with plentiful water supplies on Dartmoor, the first engineering feat of its kind, managed by none other than Sir Francis Drake, the Mayor of Plymouth at the time. Legend has it that at the opening ceremony, as water foamed down the channel, Drake rode ahead of it on his horse like an equine surfer. I can imagine the Lord Flashheart smirk on his face as he reached this spot in Crownhill, abandoned the waterway, and rode onto this flat piece of land where many carts were parked by the medieval road, for the purchasing of edible goods and sundries. Buzzing with adrenaline, he began careering around the *cart-park* on his horse, showing off to a crowd of young folk from town, performing hair-raising stunts, twirling the horse in figures of eight, leaving churned trails behind him. At times his horse almost skidded out of control, which sent up great whoops from the youngsters who sketched the event on tiny pads of parchment which they later posted on a giant message board in the city, in the hope of some *likes*. The local residents were much aggrieved by the clamour of foul language and rough music. Yet another example of English society going downhill.

Over the decades, the leat became clogged and polluted. It was lined in stone in the eighteenth century, forming the channel Dan and I have just walked. In 1911, a reservoir was built here to clean up the water before it was pumped out to the houses. The reservoir's aerator remains, a metallic grey champagne-glass fountain surrounded by a low stone ledge, upon which a solitary middle-aged woman sits in her orange B&Q apron, head bowed, her cigarette trailing smoke. I can't imagine shoppers utilise this space much, so far from the entrance, surrounded by cars and not signposted. They'd have to look for it, or stumble upon it. But who decides to wander into the centre of a car park purely to get a sense of the vista? They are here to get tiles, buy drugs or pick up a Meat Feast. Dan is an architectural historian and not even he has been to this spot until now.

In a superstore car park the space outside your car is largely invisible. You move to the store entrance as efficiently as possible. The rest of the landscape may be a bubbling lake of fire for all you care. You don't explore. You don't go to those edges where the white lines fade, loners sit in idling cars and rat traps wait for victims. Few will notice a site of historical interest in a car park, not even an engineering innovation which rescued the city from drought, created by Sir Francis Drake, Britain's favourite Elizabethan privateer. This is how his leat remains a piece of architectural history hidden in plain sight between B&Q and KFC, unloved and breathtaking.

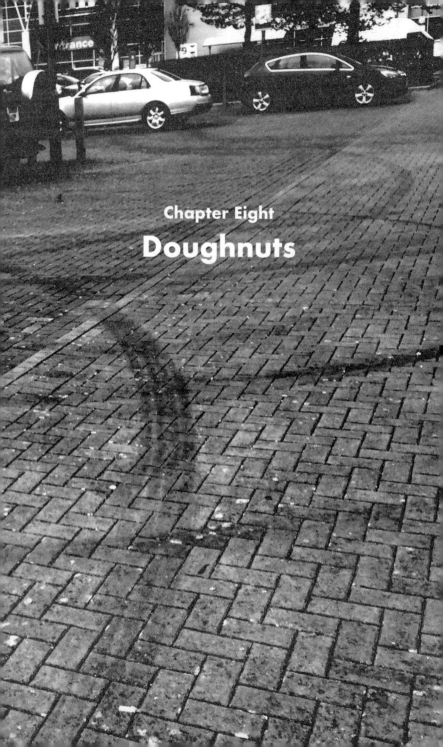

Chapter Eight
Doughnuts

A few months after I visit the Crownhill Retail Park it hosts a nocturnal gathering of around a hundred cars and five hundred people. Twenty-year-old Christopher Budd is in competition with his friend Ryan Swaddling, whom he has just seen do a cracking burnout, his car barely visible amidst clouds of smoke. Not to be outdone, Budd slams the accelerator on his red Ford Fiesta and hurtles towards Swaddling's Honda Civic. A crowd of kids on the kerb gasp in delight, raising their smartphones. Budd waggles his foot at the brake as he turns the wheel to skid free of collision, but he makes no contact with the brake pedal and his car does not stop. It does not skid. Things are no longer okay. He is in the hands of forces he cannot control. Momentum takes over. The car hits the kerb and ploughs into the crowd, knocking down sixteen spectators and flipping a teenage girl into the windscreen, shredding her face on the glass. Screams fill the night and blood flows outside B&Q. Despite this, the footage ends up on YouTube. There is no point in wasting the moment. Violence is viral and likes are currency.

That same year, a forty-seven-year-old named Tracey Ann Hernandez goes for drinks in Llanelli to celebrate her house purchase. Hours later the police catch her in the Asda car park, three sheets to the wind, merrily performing doughnuts in her Fiat, smoke billowing. She later tells the court that she lives a sober life and rarely goes out. This was a blip. A moment of madness. She does not know what made her jump behind the wheel of her car and career round an Asda at night. Neither do I. Perhaps it was the car park that led her astray. That alluring flat surface, the tantalising wideness of space, the joy of transgression. We assume that we are authors of our actions, but often we are the product of our environment, corralled by urban planners into designated commercial zones with parking limits and strict rules, slaves to direction signs, even when we feel driven to rebel against them, to attack our masters, flailing our fists against their chests. The problem isn't that one or two people occasionally go mad in car parks, it's that not enough of us go mad in car parks. Whatever her true motive, Hernandez joins the legions of lowriders, joyriders and cruisers across the country who turn car parks into stunt arenas.

In 2017, petrolheads gather for an unauthorised rally in a Tesco Extra car park in the Brislington area of Bristol, an event they advertise on social media. The air roars with the noise of hundreds of modified cars. Inside the store, staff peer out nervously as the spectators amass. The police are called. When they arrive, a woman clambers on the bonnet and spits at an officer. This sparks a downpour of bottles and stones. Reinforcements are called in, and what the police describe as 'major disorder' breaks out. The car park becomes a chaos of cop cars, modified vehicles and improvised missiles, ended only by the arrest of the bonnet-surfing woman and a dispersal notice. A year later, a crowd of two hundred descends on the Quedgeley Tesco on a Sunday evening. A disgruntled post on the *Gloucestershire Live* Facebook page moans, 'This is Gloucester, not a city from *The Fast and the Furious.*' Another rails, 'The noise is awful, the smell of burning rubber, kids being woken up by it and scaring animals.' But some defend the perpetrators. 'The nearest motorsport venue is Castle Coombe and is too costly for most but the wealthy to use,' says one commentator. 'Better the kids use the car park than terrorising the residential streets,' opines another.

Sometimes the action spills out of the car park. At a Tesco in South Queensferry, West Lothian, kids use the cash machine to withdraw bank statements that show the location and time. They leap into their cars and speed for three miles to the village of Newton, where they turn and race back to Tesco to withdraw a second statement. Here is absolute proof of their race time, down to the second. No arguments. *I win. Pay up, you prick.* With their all-night munchies, petrol pumps and cash machines, supermarket car parks are ideal starting points for these wacky races.

Bournemouth's Ferndown Tesco car park regularly buzzes with car horns, adrenaline and hardcore techno until 3.45 a.m. Robin Park Asda in Wigan is a local speedway track after sundown. 'Anything could happen walking across there at night,' complains local Mark Feagan, 'there is no security out there.' In Blackwood, Wales, eighty-five cruisers are caught revving around Asda, McDonald's and KFC in the space of an hour. For almost twenty-five years the car parks of Sainsbury's and Asda, bifurcated by the A41 on the Dome Roundabout in North Watford, have played host to wild stunts and races after the stores close. Neighbours complain about the cacophony of tyres, engine roars, whoops and cheers.

The smash of broken bottles. Phat beats from the woofers. Raucous chit-chat. *Have you got any Rizla, mate?*

From the safety of a Solihull supermarket petrol station, staff look on as a thousand people watch boy racers express their knightly instincts on a self-made drag strip, jousting with cars to screams of delight from onlookers with iPhones. In a Plymouth Morrisons one evening, Karolina Jaworeli and the young daughter of her friend are passing through the car park when they're caught in the glare of headlamps as two boy racers speed towards them. They cower in a trolley as racers circle them, whooping like cowboys, middle fingers aloft. In a Dudley Tesco on Boxing Day, cars gather in the multistorey. A VW Golf, a red Peugeot and a silver Vauxhall Corsa snake around the ramparts with a twenty-year-old woman on the bonnet until she slides off, fatally hitting her head. In a Bournemouth pub car park a thirty-year-old man shows off his driving skills to the twenty-six-year-old hairdresser he's taken on a date. His BMW ploughs into a tree, crunching the bonnet and shattering her arm. The man flees the scene, leaving the hairdresser pinned inside, weeping and bleeding.

'It's definitely the worst date I've ever been on,' she tells the *Daily Star*.

Many cruisers believe that night-racing is a legitimate use for car parks and they have a right to do it unimpeded. Their behaviour is exacerbated by confusion over the legal status of supermarket car parks. Are they classed as public roads and therefore governed by the Road Traffic Act 1988? In 2012, a woman was stopped by police for talking on her mobile as she drove through a car park. She argued in court that she was not on a public highway, so the law did not apply, but she lost the case.

A road in England and Wales is defined as 'any highway and any other road to which the public has access'. If a private car park has gates that limit access times, then it can be considered 'private' and outside of the Road Traffic Act. But if it's open to all, it is a 'route of good intention' and therefore the Act applies. This is why many retail store car parks are classed as public places by the police and why serious driving offences apply. But the law is one thing, and how a place is actually used is another.

Piston-heads feel that not only are car parks an ideal location for their hobby, but that it should be welcomed. On a forum, a commentator claims that doing stunts in car parks is 'a great way to learn car control and ideally the facilities should be made available to improve what is basically a survival skill'. He adds, 'I remember spending a couple of hours in the car park in Cobham in my Lancia, sliding around like a nutter. No Bibs showed up to tell me off.' Meanwhile, on a 'driver defence' website, a man complains:

> 'I was doing donuts in a new vehicle which I was insured for in a very large empty retail car park. Undercover police came and gave me 3 points and a 60 pound fine. They were very rude called me a dick and a few other things, stereotyped me. Also they only saw me do one donut (skid).'

His logic seems to be that it's all a matter of scale. Doing one doughnut is *fine*. You cannot police that. One doughnut could occur accidentally. Who could condemn a guy for doing one doughnut? It's insane. But any more than that, he implies, and it's okay for the police to intervene, as long as they're polite and don't make stereotypical assumptions about you being a dick, even if you are one.

In April 2017, gangster-affiliated millionaire Frankie 'Donuts' Donaldson gets his comeuppance in a Glasgow car park when a gang beats him to a bloody pulp as he leaves his car. It means he cannot appear in court later that day to be sentenced for what the *Daily Record* calls 'a horror campaign of violent domestic abuse'. Car parks attract doughnuts. But they also destroy doughnuts. It's the circle of life.

Chapter Nine

There is Something Wrong with Leyton Mills Retail Park

There's something wrong with Leyton Mills Retail Park. I didn't notice it in my East London days, long before my car park manifesto, when I'd go there with my wife to shop at B&Q. In need of a bit of wood, Rawlplugs or a thingy to fix an object to another thingy, we'd drive from Clapton across the Lea Bridge, then follow the railway lines at the back of Hackney Marsh. A solar system of mini-roundabouts slung us like space probes past a Eurostar depot, allotments and a petrol station, into a car park surrounded by chain stores (Asda, Next, Pizza Hut, KFC, Costa Coffee, TK Maxx, the usual culprits), built on a former railway goods yard.

B&Q means Boring & Quiet. They don't say that on the big orange sign, but that's what it means. I'd trail forlornly behind Emily as she searched for Polyfilla, rollers and wallpaper paste. She was good at DIY. She knew the gauges of things and what kind of paint adhered to what kind of surface. Mostly I'd glide on the trolley or mess around on my iPhone. Sometimes we'd nip into Asda afterwards to pick up food. Then it was back in the car, B&Q quickly forgotten.

That was almost a decade ago. Since then, a large portion of the ice caps have melted. One hundred and eighty million acres of rainforest have disappeared. Numerous people have died, and an even larger number have been born. The London Olympics have come and gone, its jubilant international optimism reduced to bitter xenophobia. The Hadron Collider has been activated by scientists researching the Higgs field, a force that acts on particles, giving them mass. Scientists are desperate to find stuff in the universe that we can't see so that the stuff we *can* see will start to make sense. I, too, have detected a strange energy in car parks, of which I was not aware when my wife and I frequented the Leyton Mills Retail Park, and which might make sense of what is happening to our world. If only I can keep walking and looking, I might find my Higgs boson. This is why I am on the bullet train from Ashford to Stratford International, from where I can take a leisurely walk to Leyton Mills Retail Park and get the proper measure of the place.

The post-Olympic Stratford is a neo-Soviet landscape of residential blocks and enclosed play areas. A marble wall is engraved with Tennyson's line, 'to strive, to seek, to find, and not to yield'. Street names like Liberty Bridge Road, Prize Walk and Cheering Lane are emblems of a committee-decreed Games mythology superimposed upon industrial land. Other than a couple of workers sliding poles from the back of a van, there's nobody on the streets. A threadbare green field stretches towards silent stadia, the Westfield shopping mall and scaffolded tower blocks. It's a sketch of a place waiting to happen, tainted with the melancholy that it might not. Closer to Leyton, hoardings around the 'East Village' apartments proclaim a New Neighbourhood for real people and show images of actors playing the parts of those real people. Colour pictures of the proposed communal areas have features sketched onto them: swings, benches, birdhouses and – inexplicably – hot air balloons. In Drapers Field, a playpark is bustling with kids. To make sure everything stays friendly, signs are bolted onto the concrete:

Is this your first time here? I hope you are loved for the rest of HUMAN LIFE.

Whenever you tip your head back and LAUGH, the whole street falls in LOVE with YOU.

Is everything you love FOREIGN, or are you foreign to EVERYTHING you LOVE?

I don't understand what the questions mean, or who the questioner is supposed to be. It's like the irritating copy you get on packaging that says *Please recycle me!*, buses that say *I'm not in service!* or that sad trolley I found in Plymouth's B&Q, pleading to be returned to its owner. You're supposed to imagine the consciousness of manufactured objects speaking to you, as if the constant nagging voices in your own head aren't enough to contend with.

Leyton High Road is a Victorian terrace with shops that have names like Noorul Islam Books, Nemo Shop & Fashion and Mouloudia. As I approach the retail park, the dome of TK Maxx rises like a mosque on the far side of a bridge, where loiterers smoke outside the tube station. At the bottom of some steps is a pedestrianised street leading to the car park, with Subway, TK Maxx, Pizza Hut and KFC on one side, and a row of fake independent shops on the other, their frontages painted onto an empty building. There's a pretend shop called

Your Fashion, another called Musica, its door painted ajar as if to lure you in, and a cafe called The Leyton where they've painted pretend graffiti onto the pretend exterior. An entirely fabricated boutique called Leyton Fun has a sale on, which is great fictional news. *Waltham Forest: it's happening here*, says a fake sticker on the fake door of Marshall Music.

Two real human men in matching baseball caps sit on the doorstep of the non-real Leyton Gelato ice cream parlour, drinking cans of lager. Next door is Livo Jazz – *Open daily from 5pm*. They've painted shutters onto the painted door to show that the non-existent venue is closed. At the end of the row is an alley of cans and sleeping bags. The homeless here are real enough. A sign on the wall says: *Counterfeit DVD vendors are trespassing and may be prosecuted*. This seems a bit rich bearing in mind the counterfeit street I've just walked down. Of course, the counterfeit DVD vendors no longer exist. This sign speaks to nobody.

Outside Pizza Hut is a semi-circle of steps where a woman with a taut ponytail smokes a roll-up beside an empty Fosters can, as a nervous youngster in a suit hovers nearby with leaflets for Sky Television while his older colleague encourages him by flapping his clipboard, as if to propel him on a breeze. Skilfully swerving them, I enter the car park where the wide world of retail opens out. Costa, Carphone Warehouse, Burger King, Next, Sports Direct, Currys and B&Q are arrayed down one side. Asda takes up the opposing flank, windows adorned with photographs of giant Asda people with perfect skin and hair, clapping their hands or leaping over invisible objects in well-pressed trousers. An eight-foot Asda boy stares from the window with his mouth open in surprise, like he's discovered a portal to another dimension, through which he can see tiny people looking back at him. Next to the boy is a banner advert for air freshener: *Smell the Scents of Autumn. Not the odours.* It puzzles me. The artificial smell of autumn they've created will rid us of the odours we smell in the actual autumn? Is that the idea?

All this fiction is making me queasy. It wasn't like this in the old days, looking for beading or a spirit level in B&Q. Choosing an anglepoise lamp. Picking up light bulbs. God no. We just drove in, drove out. Now that I have had a chance to take a proper look around, I understand that there is something fundamentally wrong with Leyton Mills Retail Park.

It's not what's inside the shops. It's what's happening in the car park. To the people.

They're reading papers at the bus stop. Waiting by Belisha beacons to cross the road. Sitting in cars without their engines on. Listening to the busker with the battered guitar. Milling at the Asda entrance. Watching their kids in the playground by Costa. Drinking outside pretend cafes. Skateboarding near the recycling bins. These people are not passing through. They're dwelling here, as if this is a real town. I head past B&Q but I don't go in, not even for old times' sake. I don't need to go into superstores; the car park is the place.

At the perimeter there is a steel fence scattered with debris: plastic toilet cistern, chaise longue, burst football, window frame, bottle of Ribena, sodden carrier bags. Here's where everything breaks down. Cars are few and far between. A driver eats lunch in the cab of his truck. A woman sits on the kerb with her phone. Neither acknowledge my passing. Out by the perimeter, you're not really seen, like a planet in a distant galaxy. Only the gravitational pull of your recent card payment in B&Q or Asda suggests your existence.

A sign thanks me for shopping with Asda, and another says: *Trolleys will automatically stop if taken beyond the red line.* The words 'red line' are coloured red, to make sure I know what red looks like. At the bottom of the sign, written in a cheery font, is: *Happy to help every day.* Looking over the pyracantha shrubs by the exit, I can see the allotments by the mini-roundabout, the Eurostar depot and The Shard on the skyline beyond the marshes. There is a sound of heels clopping behind me. Someone else out walking in the nether regions of the car park. It's a woman in a black coat, carrying a Next bag. She looks uncertain that she's going the right way. When she sees me, she baulks. I keep my gaze fixed on the city skyline, so as not to embarrass her. As she reaches the *trolleys will automatically stop* sign, she grinds to a halt, confused.

'Excuse me,' she says.

'Yes?'

'Which way's Costa?'

It's a strange question. She only has to turn around to see. I raise my finger and point.

'Back there…'

She nods curtly and returns to the car park, flicking her hair into place, weaving between cars. Light shimmers on metal at her passing, as if she's disturbing sheets of dark matter, then she's gone, if she was ever here at all. I think about the Hadron Collider. *There is stuff in the universe we cannot see.* Perhaps B&Q doesn't stand for Boring & Quiet but Boson & Quark. Perhaps the store is manifesting shoppers in its Higgs field. Apparitions that dwell only in this park of facsimiles.

In which case, what does that make me?

To continue my journey, I must pass the *trolleys will automatically stop* sign. I'm oddly uncertain about what might happen if I try. Across the road, a man and woman in overalls stare at me through the slats of the allotment fence. Worried about something I cannot quite put my finger on, I step towards the red line.

Chapter Ten
Animal Instincts

There is unrest in the car park. People want their shopping done, and they want it done quickly, without impediment by those they deem to be lesser-skilled in the ways of parking, or underserving of their respect: too female, too old, too young, too foreign-looking, too poor.

An elderly man takes an age to reverse park his Ford Ka while a bald bloke in a white van behind him drums the steering wheel impatiently. Get some new specs, grandad, or get off the road. Shouldn't there be an age limit for driving? The state of this country. He turns up Ed Sheeran on his stereo. 'I never knew you were the someone waiting for meeeeee,' he bellows through the open window.

In the next row, a young female driver almost scratches the paint on a middle-aged bank manager's velocity-red Mazda RX8 as she pulls up beside him and opens her door too far. He's apoplectic with rage. 'Silly bitch!' he yells. Women shouldn't even be allowed a bloody license. Their brains are wired differently, lacking in spatial awareness. He read it somewhere online. There's a baby in the back seat of her car so she should be using the 'parent-and-child' parking spaces, that's what they're there for – not that he agrees with *that* stupid system either, as those enlarged parent-child things swallow up space that could be used for more cars, and anyway most of them are taken up by parents with hulking great kids who don't need buggies. The whole thing is a shambles and yet again it's normal hard-working men like himself who get penalised. Not that men have rights any more. Bloody feminazis. He has a good mind to get out and give her a slap – baby or no baby. Heck, the fatherless little brat might even learn something from it.

Meanwhile, at the parent-and-child parking, a mother of three in an animal-print Zara top chews gum like a speed freak and yells blue murder at a tubby twenty-something with a bowl haircut and Superman T-shirt who stands blithely with an overflowing shopping bag in the spot she's trying to access. Probably special needs or something, but it's not her problem, is it? 'Facking 'ell, shift your fat arse.'

Behind her, engine idling, is a pensioner who wants to access the disabled area a little further up. What's the silly cow shouting about? *Get a move on.* The elderly man shakes his head in dismay. She looks African. Probably claiming benefits, and that's why his pension's barely enough to keep him alive. Besides, how come she's got her kids with her? He thought it was school hours or he wouldn't have come to get some bread at this time of day. Children never seem to go to school any more. You get a holiday for everything now, and half of them bunk off to smoke crack pipes in the car park, blaring awful music from their phones. Then they piss on his dahlias on the way home. Everything's going downhill. Uncontrolled immigration, that's what's caused it, and now he's got to wait while one of these incomers dithers around. He's been coming here for twenty years and there are too many cars now for the size of the place. Too many people, that's the problem. Overpopulation. But you can't say *sterilisation* in public without someone getting upset. Is this what his generation fought a world war to win? Not that he was born until 1948, but still, his dad was in the war, albeit he couldn't fight because of a knee problem. Anyway, he's sick of this, really he is.

Almost as angry is the woman at the other end of the car park who's on her knees analysing how much of the neighbouring vehicle's wheel is over the white line. It's the entire tyre! The vehicle's parked at an absurd angle. She's going to have to clamber in through the passenger seat. God knows how much room she has available to reverse out. She might be blocked in and she's got a doctor's appointment in twenty minutes. Some people have no respect. No consideration for others. They just do what they want. She's a good mind to pull out her keys out and scrape the metalwork. That'll show them.

Every minute of every opening hour, a car pulls in, a car pulls out, a space is filled, another vacated. There is potential for violence compressed within these small, mundane actions, like the nuclear energy stored inside an atom. The parking system is simple enough, you place your car between the lines in the correctly allocated zones, but there is entropy – that spillage of disorder and chaos around the edges, when things go slightly out of kilter, thanks to natural human error. We are not machines like our cars. We are animals with deep primal instincts, hormonal urges and behavioural idiosyncrasies. We don't always fit into allocated spaces. And it only takes the smallest mistake for violence to be unleashed.

Outside a Bedfordshire ASDA, sixty-five-year-old Alan Watts is waiting in his Range Rover for his wife to emerge when he spots sixty-four-year-old Alan Holmes putting his shopping bags into his vehicle, which is parked in a disabled bay.

'You look like you need a wheelchair,' sneers Watts from his passenger window.

Holmes, a cancer survivor, whose wife possesses a blue disabled badge, takes offence and approaches Watt to remonstrate. In the ensuing fracas, Watts punches Holmes in the face twice. He topples to the ground, cracking his skull. Holmes later dies. Sentencing him to manslaughter, the judge tells Watts that his actions are 'akin to road rage'.

A YourParkingSpace.co.uk survey has revealed that one in ten people have been threatened with physical violence in car parks. There's a psychological reason for this. An American study, *Territorial Defense in Parking Lots: Retaliation Against Waiting Drivers*, shows that when drivers are about to leave a parking space, while another car waits to enter that same space, they exhibit protective territorial behaviours. This includes procrastination techniques such as faffing with the seat belt, selecting a radio station, checking their phone or messing with the air conditioning. The waiting car is a predatory threat to the parked driver, stimulating primal urges in their reptilian brain. This gets worse if the waiting driver parps their horn impatiently, an act of aggression that will cause the leaver to tarry even longer. The study found that, for men, the status of the waiting car is influential. For instance, if a Lexus is the waiting vehicle, men drive away sooner than they might for a Nissan Micra.

This behaviour runs contrary to our conscious desire to leave the superstore, and makes no practical sense, but we are animals, governed largely by our instincts. It is these instincts that retail businesses rely on for sales. In 1974, Philip Koetler wrote a paper on 'atmospherics as a marketing tool' for the *Journal of Retailing*, in which he described how colours, smells, sounds and surface textures put consumers into an emotionally suggestive state. In a 2010 article for *The Independent*, Simon Usborne described the techniques used by Tesco, Sainsbury's, Asda and Morrisons to entice more spending. 'For the designers of the modern store,' he wrote, 'shoppers are lab rats with trolleys, guided through a maze of aisles by the promise of rewards they never knew they sought.' Endcaps on aisles are filled with special offers that trigger the bargain-hunting instinct, that fear of missing out, even when the savings don't quite stack up if you crunch the numbers. The wood effect in the wine aisle inspires feelings of authenticity and tradition, while the baking smells wafting through the store suggest freshness. Essentials like milk and bread are placed at the back, so that the customer must run a gauntlet of temptation from items they had no previous intention to buy. Music by popular artists entices the shopper to linger, slipping special offers into the mesmeric mix. Near the checkouts, 'impulse areas' contain irresistible treats like chocolate, crisps and sweets, stimulating the saliva glands. With their logical thought patterns bypassed, shoppers return to the car park in heightened emotional states, brimming with primal urges, feeling remorse that they've spent too much on things they don't need. Then, just as they're packing the car to head home, they're assailed by ignorant incomers who want their space. It's irritating. An afront. They will leave when *they* are ready and not before.

What's extraordinary is that the angry car park user is aware that the parking space in which they sit is not really theirs. It belongs to the store. They have been granted temporary permission to park for the purposes of spending money in that store, lining the pockets of a giant corporation and enriching its shareholders. Yet their instinct is to defend this borrowed space, and with their fists if they have to. A similar phenomenon occurs in pubs, when strangers linger near your table as you're about to finish your drink, hoping to get your seat. *Vultures!* you think, taking a little longer to get your belongings together, feeling that the table is somehow yours and that the waiting people don't deserve it.

In car parks, emotions are further intensified by our toxic relationship with the automobile. As poet Heathcote Williams wrote in 'Autogeddon' (1991):

From the moment the driver
Settles behind the wheel
Stress readings increase
As the driver's body is slowly marinated with
adreno-toxins

In what is already an accident-prone landscape, car park users are psychologically on edge. Professor Leon James, an expert in road rage at the University of Hawaii, says, 'Behind the wheel you assume another personality that is much more geared towards warfare[5]'. We feel that our car is an extension of our body, so that when threatened by another car, we react as we would to an invasion of our personal space. The difference is that when strangers invade our space as pedestrians, we don't resort to aggression. If someone accidentally blocks our way on the pavement we engage in a polite 'no you first' dance,

5   *Telegraph*, 14 Oct 2006, https://www.telegraph.co.uk/motoring/road-safety/2743699/Road-rage-what-makes-us-do-it.html

often accompanied by a chuckle or eyeball roll. When we go through a doorway at the same time as a stranger, a sense of embarrassed awkwardness leads us to apologise, or laugh off the situation. Not so inside in the steel shell of a car, the power of acceleration at your feet, hormonal excretions swimming through your bloodstream towards the crocodilian brain stem, stimulating flight or fight reactions. The 'no you first' dance becomes 'fuck off and die, you wanker'. When this spills into real violence, it's known as 'Intermittent explosive disorder' – where an otherwise reasonable person uses sudden, aggressive behaviour, out of proportion to the offence.

Sometimes the attacker rages not against other individuals, but against segments of society they feel have aggrieved them. There is YouTube footage of a forty-four-year-old man jumping on top of an empty police car parked outside Sainsbury's in Deptford, south London. He stomps back and forth, his female companion pleading for him to stop, then slides off the car and smashes the rear window, hauling out items and whacking them against the vehicle. People stand around watching, doing nothing to stop him, possibly for entertainment, a vicarious enjoyment of the violent act, or subconscious admiration.

In 2016, retired handyman Ethem Orhon rampages through the car park of a Sainsbury's in Hampton, stabbing four women. The previous day he felt humiliated when police strip-searched him after arresting him for possession of a blade. As soon as he is let out on bail he returns home, grabs a Leatherman knife, then heads to Sainsbury's because, as he later admits in court, it is the most crowded place he knows. He feels as if he is acting via remote control, he insists in a police interview.

'I became a different person... There was one thought in my mind, which was: go home, grab the spare knife and assault people... I feel I had to do it and finish the job. I had to obey the order.' Despite his mental health problems, the judge decides that he was in control of his decision and jails him for twenty years for attempted murder and grievous bodily harm.

A similar psychological flip-out occurs when sixty-year-old Linda Glover leaves a twenty-four-hour Northumberland Asda at 1 a.m., clambers behind the wheel and begins to ram her car into vehicles, bollards and trolleys. When the police arrive, she explains that she was attempting to kill herself, but later in court her lawyer insists that she cannot remember anything about the event. He says: 'This has been a traumatic experience for her and she has no explanation for what she did. She is so concerned about it that she has not driven since.'

These are isolated incidents of individual rage. But there is potential for the car park to instigate mass hysteria and violence, the most famous example being the Battle of IKEA in 2005, when a crowd of 6,000 gathered outside a store in Edmonton, north London, at midnight for a sale. IKEA had reduced their £325 sofas to £49 and the bargain stirred powerful desires in the crowd, their anticipation fermenting in the crucible of the car park. There was a festive mood as music played, fire-eaters performed and stilt-walkers strutted across the tarmac. According to a crowd member, Sol Sheikh, when interviewed on GMTV, the fun atmosphere soured after 10 p.m. when 'slowly but steadily, madness descended on the crowd', with people attempting to jump the queue, scrabbling for pole position. In a dramatic flourish, the store manager, Tom Williams, carried out the Swedish 'good luck' tradition of cutting a log to open the event. As the doors slid apart, the crowd surged, bodies jamming the entrance, stumbling through the doorway, falling and tripping. A mass of people in the car park fought to get in. Chaos erupted in the soft furnishings department. A civil servant, Karyn Christian, later told the press: 'There were people diving on sofas and lying on them and others pulling them off with their feet. There were people tugging at two different sides of the same sofa and shouting "mine, mine". It was just horrible. People were going crazy.' Animal instincts took over. A man threatened a woman with a mallet. Another dragged a sofa from a woman's trolley near the checkout. As the violence escalated, the security guards stood by, helpless. Forty minutes later, the store closed and twenty people were hospitalised with heat exhaustion and injuries. In the car park, a man in his twenties lay with stab wounds. Remarkably, police declared that the stabbing was not related to the consumer riot, but to a gang dispute, meaning that at the same time as crazed shoppers tore each other to shreds over cheap sofas, gang members were bloodletting over territory, all in the same car park.

Only three years later, failing to learn from the Battle of IKEA, Currys held a sale in their West Midlands Megastore, offering satnavs with a ninety per cent discount, a third off Playstations, and TVs at half price. The store was set to open at 8.30 a.m. but people began arriving at 8 p.m. the previous night, with sleeping bags, flasks, hats and scarves. The store gave them tea and coffee, playing films to keep them entertained. By 5 a.m. there were 3,000 people present. Tensions rose as newcomers pushed in. Arguments and scuffles broke out. On the M6 a seven-mile queue stretched in both directions, with police brought in to control the traffic. As pressure increased in the car park, the store opened early. A stampede ensued, shoppers scrapping in the aisles and stealing goods from each other. An anonymous Currys worker told a journalist: 'One woman loaded a forty-inch TV onto her trolley, turned around to get something else and by the time she looked back it had been stolen.'

When asked to comment on the events, a store manager explained: 'Now more than ever people are looking for good value.'

It's an odd thing to say in the aftermath of carnage, but perhaps we should embrace the animalistic urges of the populace, give them the value they crave, offer them more things to buy, more choice, more space, more parking. Let it all out. Give them space to dream, to fight, to kill.

Liberation through parking!

Chapter Eleven

The Joy of Parking

In the mid-nineties, my then-girlfriend lived in Bristol while I worked in a radio station in Cardiff, on the other side of the Severn Bridge. She was a traffic and travel presenter for the region, circling the skies in a plane, issuing live reports during peak-time shows. The station's output was streamed into our offices, a mix of bombastic DJ links, local adverts (many of them written by me) and a rotation of audience-tested hits by The Spice Girls, Cast, The Beautiful South, Reef and Cheryl Crow, including the worst song ever made, 'Breakfast at Tiffany's' by Deep Blue Something, which played on the hour, every hour, and filled me with deep blue despair. But I could cope because every now and then my girlfriend's voice emerged from the slurry of audio excrement to sweeten my ears.

'There's slow-moving traffic on the A4232 outbound but otherwise the roads are clear this morning.'

'A truck collision has closed down two lanes of the M4 Westbound and queues are building up from Junction 26'.

'We're getting reports of black ice on the A470 towards Castle Coch.'

Beautiful.

I spent many weekends at her shared flat in Bristol until she dumped me for her co-presenter in the traffic and travel plane. It was a devastating turn of events. As I walked through the city to work each morning, I could see her plane circling the skies above me. I imagined the two of them inside, touching each other's knees. Her traffic reports, piped through a speaker above my desk, became a torment. 'After an earlier accident on the A48, the congestion is clearing and it looks like traffic is back on the move.' *Oh yes, I bet it is, you pair of bastards*.

Not long after this heartbreak I left Cardiff for London, but I would return to Bristol occasionally to visit my brother, who had found work in a Harvester pub in Bradley Stoke, a suburban area to the north of the city, nestled within a triangle formed by the M5 and M4, where former farmland had been turned into overspill housing estates and trading estates, threaded by mini-roundabouts and serviced by a parkway. Wedged between two motorways, bifurcated by the Swansea to London railway line, it felt like a place on the way to somewhere else, from which you might depart rather than go, more connective tissue than beating heart.

It's December, and I've returned to this windswept outer ring of Bristol to visit the Cribb's Causeway Retail Park. It's an intriguing name, implying a strong topographical connection. The legend goes that 'Cribb' comes from Tom Cribb, a local bare-knuckle boxer, but the truth is that this area was called Cribb before his birth in 1781. Nobody knows who this original Cribb family might have been, or why they gave their name to a causeway. A book by Veronica Smith, entitled *The Street Names of Bristol – Their Origins and Meaning*, suggests that 'Crib' might even refer to a manger, something that adds resonance to the festive season in which I am visiting. The causeway itself was once a Roman road leading from a settlement called Portus Abonae (Sea Mills) to Colonia Nervia Glevensium (Gloucester), a retirement town for legionnaires. Today it's called the A4018, a road connecting up with the M5 motorway, the main conduit of traffic from the Midlands to the South-West. As a confluence of multiple transport routes, the causeway is an attractive proposition for commercial developers.

By the end of the 1960s, the increased affordability of cars meant that retail businesses had to supply enough parking spaces, making it harder to find new locations in town centres. So they started to seek sites outside of towns and cities where they could design bigger stores, with more choice under one roof, and vast car parks with petrol stations, cafes and restaurants. While many were relieved to see new retail developments move away from their towns, critics accused the new superstores of destroying high-street trade, and it was the lure of ample parking and 'all-in-one' convenience that was to blame. In 1976, as this trend took hold, the go-ahead was given for a new hypermarket on Cribb's Causeway, at the junction of the A4018 and the M5. Other stores quickly sprung up around it, each with their attendant parking areas, and so the Cribbs Causeway Retail Park was born. In 1998, the Mall was opened: a gigantic block of high-end chain stores hunkered within the older retail network, a cuckoo in another bird's nest.

I am here because its website makes an offer I cannot refuse. *Experience the joy of 7,000 free parking spaces.*

In this statement they have stimulated my deepest desires. Because while few people in this world would shun an opportunity to experience joy, my preferred joy is a very specific genre of joy, the kind you only get from 7,000 free parking spaces. Although I'll admit that there is some ambiguity in the statement. Does the joy come from parking free of charge, or from the knowledge that 7,000 parking spaces are freely available? Or is it clever wordplay that refers to both meanings? In which case, there is more to the sentence than is contained within it. Rarely can a shopping mall car park's core mission statement have such a sense of mystery. Of poetry.

Whatever their intention, I am certain that the authors of the statement believed that to experience the joy of 7,000 parking spaces you would need a car to park. To enjoy 7,000 car parking spaces that you don't need and cannot possibly use is perverted. But that is what I am about to do. Worse, I have no intention of spending any money at Cribb's Causeway. I will enjoy their parking spaces without parking and without rewarding them with a purchase for their efforts. I won't even sneak inside to buy a sandwich. It's everything they don't want. I'm an aberration, a freeloader taking the piss. However, it is Christmas and I am but a humble traveller, like one of the shepherds who visited the Christ child, travelling by foot to pay homage to what they have built. They cannot begrudge me that.

To reach Cribb's Causeway from Parkway station, the taxi driver weaves me through Bradley Stoke, Little Stoke and Patchway, onto the edge of the Severn Escarpment. I stare out at the grey-green blur of bungalows, industrial units, bus shelters and new-build housing estates. We're far away from the trendy mural zones of Stokes Croft and Montpelier, where bohemians hang out in coffee houses and eat poppy seed muffins. This is another Bristol. Commuter belt Bristol. Functional Bristol. Hipster-free Bristol. 'Do you often get people taking taxis from the station to Cribb's Causeway?' I ask.

'Not really,' says the taxi driver. 'People drive or get the bus – it has its own stop. Besides, most want picking up *after* they've got their shopping.'

I ask him to drop me off a little way before we reach the entrance, which he finds strange, and he asks me twice if I am sure. 'Oh, it's fine, I'll enjoy the walk in,' I chirp, stepping onto a scrubby strip of road beside the entrance to the Gregory Distribution depot. As he zooms away, I approach a roundabout near the access road to the rear of Cribb's Causeway Mall, which I can see looming beyond a sparse treeline. In the centre of the roundabout is a mound – possibly a knoll, or barrow – from which rises a large menhir. 'Also Sprach Zarathustra' strikes up as a cloud bank splits in two, revealing the winter sun, and the monolith turns from grey to golden. Out here on the Roman road, marking the entrance to the Mall car park, this faux-Neolithic standing stone sculpture suggests that we have progressed from the worship of the old gods into a brave new dawn of commerce, fossil fuel combustion and convenient parking. It reminds me of the statue of the Ancestor on his knees outside the Holiday Inn at the Solstice Retail Park in Amesbury. The implication of artworks like these is that from the time humans learned to use tools, capitalism became inevitable. In the moment an ape-like biped first used a flint hammer to hack an animal carcass into something a group of people could eat, a line of causality stretched all the way to the construction of places like Cribb's Causeway, where technologies driven by petroleum, coal and plastics allow for the vast distribution of products for consumption, a system which must continue for the sake of economic growth. We are told there is no other option, no alternative to the organisation of society than the one we have, an idea encouraged by the sorts of vested corporate interests represented inside the mall. The stone says this is progress. The stone points to an implied future. The stone wants arrivals at Cribb's Causeway to feel thankful for how far we've come. All I can think of is the unfolding global environmental catastrophe in which we live and how my children's children could be forced to fight with sticks over the carcinogenic, nutrient-stripped remnants of the sixth great extinction. This standing stone in a roundabout between the food distribution centre and shopping complex, in farmland concreted over for the passage of automobiles, is the perfect artwork for the Anthropocene. It does not represent how far we have come, but how far we will fall. It is the gateway to the abyss.

I pass beneath the sign for Cribb's Causeway Retail Park into what looks more like an airport car park than a superstore car park – vast and sprawling, zoned with letters, leading to the rear wall of the mall, bearing the fabled name: Marks & Spencer. My walk begins in area H, a largely empty outer fringe with sections controlled by rusting barriers, stiffly raised, awaiting a time of crisis, potentially the kind of riot experienced at IKEA. Between the parking bays are strips of pyracantha shrubs with red berries, snakes of barbed wire, the occasional stray trolley on the verge, and CCTV cameras on high poles. Two men chat outside a white van, parked near an empty double-decker bus. A car rumbles by, as I walk contrary to the direction suggested by the white arrow, circling the car park edge bordered by shrubs in a rolling wave of topiary, a frozen green sea, beyond which I can see more Bronze Age barrows on mini-roundabouts. I descend stone steps to the car park for Marks & Spencer's food hall. A surprisingly pretty path through tall hedgerows leads to the entrance, where billboards tell ethical jokes:

We believe in sustainable fishing
Hook, line & sinker.

Ha ha ha ha.

Our coffee won't leave a bitter taste in your
mouth.
It's Fairtrade.

Ho ho ho!

There's nothing woolly about our
commitment to animal welfare.

This one I don't get. Most animals are not woolly. It only works if it refers to sheep. However, these signs are not designed to be thought about in any depth. I hate the phrase 'virtue signalling' because it's a weaponised Orwellian phrase used by right-wingers to devalue any statement by someone who supports the fair treatment of others, but if there is such a thing as virtue signalling, it's these adverts: they erroneously signal that there is a moral consciousness to this multinational corporation. Whether the flippant wordplay bears scrutiny is of no importance. It just needs you to know – before you buy your cellophane-wrapped apples and factory-farmed pulled pork microwave ready meal – that Marks & Spencer cares about life on earth, whether it's a sheep, salmon or Peruvian farmer. They also care about humans, particularly those affluent elderly customers who enjoy the food range for its sophisticated flavours as much as they enjoy the store interior for its lack of raucous Lidl riff-raff. This zone behind the food hall is well cultivated, with benches placed within the car park, offering a place for folk to rest their weary legs en route to their cars, much like the retired Roman legionnaires might have done on this very spot, en route to Colonia Nervia Glevensium, the retirement settlement where they would finish their days in doddery respite, remembering scenes from their youth – for instance, walking though barley fields towards their wives, then later avenging those who murdered their wives, something involving a dalliance with a boy in a bath house, and that time when their syphilitic friend married a horse. To help the contemporary legionnaire (human resources managers, headteachers, chartered accountants, car showroom receptionists, recruitment consultants) contemplate their final pasture, there's a free-standing advertising billboard for Westbury Fields Retirement Village. This is not just a car park, this is a thoughtfully landscaped, socially conscious Marks & Spencer car park.

Around the corner of Marks & Spencer is the official entrance to the Mall, a huge block of square grey panels with a frontage of glass and steel, including two arched cantilevered glass canopies, one at the apex and another directly over the revolving hotel-style doors. I'm taken aback by the sight of a traditional red postbox, stark on the paving slabs against the car park backdrop, its intimations of a British village weirdly incongruous. This is no relic of something that was here before, no remnant of a former community standing firm against the march of time; this location was, as they say, *all fields*.

The postbox is a reassuring signifier of authenticity placed here as a psychological tactic more than for its utility. Even odder is the silver and pink Disney palace directly in front of the Mall, next to a Victorian carousel ringed by giant candy canes, plastic deer adorning the entrance, sullen parents with snot-faced toddlers queuing to go in. A poor cover version of The Pogues' 'Fairytale of New York' blares from an ice rink where parents push children on bright orange seals. The odour of sausage, cheese and onion from the Bavarian food hut blends with exhaust fumes. Christmas lights extend from the entrance down a walkway lined with benches, an ornamental fissure of water running through the centre towards spurting fountains overlooking a roundabout. It's only when I turn and look up the walkway that I appreciate the scale of the Mall, an impressive glass atrium with two tall palm trees behind the window of the second floor. Heading back along the water feature, the Mall grows and expands before me, like a magnificent cathedral. I skirt around the Christmas attractions and make my way along the frontage, where the name John Lewis is emblazoned in white sans serif font, until I reach the end of the building.

From this lofty vantage point I can see the rest of the retail park spread out below in a deep bowl of walkways, car parks, warehouse roofs, store signs, street lamps and floodlights stretching to the yellow lights of a Morrisons and a wooded escarpment which carries the M5. Walkways with steel balustrades spiral to underground parking lit by strip lighting. Cars snake around ramparts, disappear into subterranean chambers and emerge onto roofs, engine noise a perpetual atonal chant. There is so much parking that

Gareth E. Rees

I cannot quite take it all in. Even though I know that there are precisely 7,000 parking spaces here, enjoyable ones at that, it feels infinite. The Escher lithograph of parking. Parking in a dream where you try to find a spot and it's always full but there's another zone of free spaces ahead, so you drive to that, but find it is suddenly full, before you see there's another parking area, and another one, and another one, and you keep going, watching the skin on your hands grow wrinkly against the steering wheel and arthritis throb in your knees, gums retracting, hair falling out, life passing you by, never quite parking, never quite getting there, but never quite leaving, until your whole life is a car park and the only reason you now fear death is that the afterlife might be a car park too. I am awestruck. If the Mall is the main temple, where the most important retail priests reign, this is its attendant city. For this isn't just one retail park, but a network of interconnected retail parks, like the boroughs of London. To the side of the Mall is a dry concrete moat, planted with shrubs, over which a pedway leads to a Halfords and Kiddicare in a contemporary building with a steep angled roof, reminiscent of a Scandinavian church. Below it is the Centaurus Retail Park, a shabbier place, the likes of which you might get on the outskirts of a boring town ring road, looking a little like a grainy photo from the 1980s. These older retail areas contain lower-brow shops than those found inside the Mall, like Currys, B&Q, Asda and McDonald's. The shrubs are sparser and drier. There's no money for topiary, ceremonial water features or Bavarian sausage shacks down here. The parking looks a lot less enjoyable than advertised on the website, although certainly as plentiful. I could keep walking through retail parks, I expect, all the way to the treeline, but something makes me stop.

Rising from a busy roundabout is a massive grass-covered cone earthwork with a metallic nipple at its apex. It dwarfs the dimensions of the menhir on the mini-roundabout I saw coming into the Mall. With its bastard fusion of steel and soil, this futuristic monolith is a manifestation of the utopian future implied by the standing stone. What function is served by this giant tit, I have no idea. Perhaps the High Priests of the Mall are huddled inside, watching the car park on CCTV, picking out sacrificial victims to slay. Its location on the busiest roundabout in the complex means that it is there to be viewed from vehicles passing at speed, never traversed on foot, caressed by human hands or scrutinised up close. Perhaps this structure is here to remind us that there are things about this car park we can never understand, and should never try. Really, it is not even a car park but an interconnected system of transit, commerce, entertainment and parking, hard to define and impossible to comprehend in its entirety. We can see the parts but not the whole. The Cribb's Causeway Retail Park is an unknowable quantum object that transcends time, from the Neolithic standing stone to the 1980s shops to the cathedral mall to this futuristic beacon at the centre of it all. And this place is just one tiny piece of the globalised economic system, which is equally unknowable, beyond any single human's control, yet which controls our daily lives, giving us food and clothing, heat and shelter. We have no choice but to live in it, and try our best to enjoy the 7,000 parking spaces, worship the religion of everlasting growth on a finite planet and bow down to this mysterious crypto-pyramid.

Gareth E. Rees

But I will not bow. I will brave the heavy traffic. I will climb the cone. God help me, I may be the first Cribb's Causeway visitor to do so since the being who constructed it. There may be sniper rifles trained on me from the upper windows of John Lewis. There may be creatures inside the steel nipple, preparing for my abduction and ritual slaughter. But I will climb and keep climbing. And when I reach the top I will look upon the world with fresh eyes and see truly the state of this bloody place[6].

6   After a little consideration I decided not to climb up the tit.

Chapter Twelve

Harm Egress

On a sunny bank holiday in May 2017, Colin Horner drives his three-year-old son into Balloo Retail Park in Bangor, County Down, and parks near Sainsbury's. They've not been in this coastal town long. Horner, a leading figure in the Loyalist movement, recently fled his home in Carrickfergus, Country Antrim, after his friend, Geordie Gilmore, was shot dead in a feud between rival paramilitary groups. He doesn't want to be next.

At 3 p.m., shopping complete, Horner buckles his son into the back seat of their SUV and steps towards the passenger door. It's a busy day, with customers streaming to and from their vehicles. From the throng emerges a masked man. He approaches Horner's SUV and speaks to him briefly. Horner begs desperately for his life before the gunman pumps six rounds into him, crumpling to the floor in a heap in front of his son. An eyewitness tells *The Mirror*: 'We were in the shop when shooting started outside and staff heard some bangs and started evacuating us very quickly. Outside the man was lying on the ground covered in blood.' The assassin is nowhere to be seen. He has vanished into the crowd amidst the hysteria, leaving the car park in a Ford Mondeo, later abandoning its burned-out wreck on a country road.

Superintendent Brian Kee tells the media that the gunman 'showed total disregard for the safety of the public, including other children, who were in the car park at the time of the attack.' Of course, the public location was very much in the assassin's mind. A surveillance vehicle driven by an accomplice had watched Horner leave his house that morning, then followed his car around town. When Horner parked outside Sainsbury's, the assassination was called in. It was perfect. Amidst the bustle of an oblivious crowd, the gunman could surprise his victim at close range and use the ensuing commotion to conceal his escape. The supermarket car park was chosen deliberately as the spot in which to murder Colin Horner. And his killers were not the first to think this way.

In 2010, gangster father-of-two Kevin 'Gerbil' Carroll arrives at the Asda in Robroyston, Glasgow, to purchase two guns from an associate. He sits in the back seat while being driven by a young man named John Bonner. As they stop, a Volkswagen Golf pulls up and two masked men get out. Bonner scrambles through the passenger door and tumbles to the ground, car keys in his fist. He later claims that he accidentally locked the car by remote control as he fell, trapping Carroll inside with no chance of escape. The gunmen shoot Carroll five times in the head before they pile back into the Golf and speed away. Four days previously, Kevin Carroll had tried to murder Eddie Lyons Jr, the son of a rival gang's boss. Lyons survived, thanks to a bulletproof vest. In retaliation, the family arranged the Asda ambush. Forensic tests show that the gun used to murder Carroll was used by Carroll himself during a hit in 2007. This gun was stolen from him, then offered to him for sale, then used to shoot him to death.

Car Park Life

Car parks are ostensibly safe public spaces in which rivals can meet to thrash out a dispute, but this sense of security is an illusion. Car parks are a blind spot, a public place in which the public will barely notice you. A hub in which characters of all classes, ethnicities and psychological states can mingle freely without standing out, in which lingering for no reason is commonplace. A surveillance zone in which the CCTV cameras rarely operate or catch anything clear enough for prosecution. There is no reason why shooting or stabbing someone to death cannot happen in the glare of floodlights or bright sunshine among consumer hordes. It is often advantageous. Which is why car parks are a popular site of retribution, in which vengeance is carried out.

In 2003, jealous teen Andrew Dean Bateman drives his ex-girlfriend to a Lidl in Swansea and blasts her head with a sawn-off shotgun.

In 2013, Christopher Maze turns up at the door of his ex-girlfriend's father, Mark Maslen-Leese, and offers him a lift into town. The two men have a fractious relationship, but Maze accepts the offer. When the car pulls into Caversham's Hills Meadow Car Park, Maze produces a knife and slashes Maslen-Leese's neck, saying, 'There you go, you can have that.' Maslen-Leese staggers from the car, followed by Maze, who pushes him over and begins to kick him almost to death. Miraculously, he survives to tell a tale that puts Maze behind bars.

In a Prescot retail park, two men in their late twenties, Gerard Childs and Stephen Price, encounter Jonathan Fitchett outside JD Sports. Childs and Fitchett are on bad terms. After an angry exchange, Childs punches

Fitchett. Price joins in and within fifteen seconds Fitchett is unconscious with a ruptured artery in his skull, brain bleeding, heart in seizure.

In 2016, twenty-year-old Carl Gregory enters the car park of Broadstairs Shopping Centre where he meets John Dixon and Chris Pollard. The boys argue over insults which Carl Gregory has posted on Facebook. A fight breaks out, during which Dixon puts Carl in a stranglehold until he goes limp. Gregory dies lying in his girlfriend's arms.

Outside a Lidl in 2017, Gillian Zvomuya is found with fatal stab wounds. Her husband, the suspected killer, bleeds on the seat next to her.

Most telling of all is the disappearance from a car park of a Bradford car dealer named Sajid Saddique. On Valentine's Day in 2007, he informs his wife that he needs to nip out to the bank. It's the last time she ever sees him. His Volkswagen is later discovered in the car park of Asda in Shipley. After years of police investigation, there's no sign of Saddique. A couple of prime suspects are said to owe Saddique a lot of money, but there is not enough evidence to charge them. The police say that it's likely he was overpowered, bundled into a vehicle and driven to another location to be killed. But nobody aside from the culprits will ever know what happened in that car park, even though the events must have occurred in broad daylight during open hours, in view of other people, whether they comprehended it or not.

My research throws up endless stories of violent confrontations, robberies and beatings in supermarket car parks. The eighty-three-year-old war veteran shoved against his car, robbed of his wallet in daylight as he cries out to shoppers for help that never comes. The thirty-four-year-old man who slams an axe into another man's head in a Tesco car park. The men in balaclavas who press a gun against a woman's chest outside a supermarket in Wellingborough. The victim found drenched in blood in the entrance of the Gosport Tesco at 6.30 a.m. These stories are warping my perspective, filling my widescreen view of car parks with mutilated bodies, shattered glass and unhinged maniacs. It's hard to look upon the everyday car park without seeing blood, without feeling as if something terrible is about to kick off. As I walk through them, I begin to see evidence of murderous deeds and sinister intent in even the most bucolic locations. This explains what happens to me in Caerphilly.

———————

I'm in Wales for the launch of a new issue of *The Lonely Crowd*, a Welsh literary quarterly in which one of my stories appears. The story is about a car park attendant who notices that the position of abandoned trolleys correlates with an ominous astrological pattern, warning of catastrophe. But is the car park really sending her messages of impending doom, or is she reading too much into things? I wrote the story after repeatedly asking myself the same question. A few attendees seem to enjoy the extract, although it's hard to tell whether they're laughing with me or at me. Nobody makes a purchase from the optimistically stacked box of my previous works, and at the end of the evening I'm forced to lift it in front of the other writers, trying not to groan with the weight of unsold literature.

After the gig I stay at the flat of an old friend from my days at Red Dragon FM. We drink too much beer and the next morning I feel fragile, yet determined to do some book research while I'm in Wales. Caerphilly is only a ten-minute drive north from his flat, and with a bit of Google hunting I discover that there's a Morrisons near the castle. A picturesque Welsh car park, nestled in the Rhymney Valley on a warm May day. It sounds gentle enough.

Descending into the town, Caerphilly Castle is majestic in the morning haze, a Norman military compound crawling with ivy, surrounded by a moat. I find a space to park nearby and cross from the castle grounds to a pedestrian shopping street with faux-Victorian lamps, bandstand and clock topped by a weather vane in the shape of the castle. This is Castle Court, the website of which declares: 'Much more than a shopping centre, we are the social hub of our local community.' It has the air of an independent high street, even though it's a regeneration scheme with the same mix of popular chain stores as you might find in any shopping centre in any town in the UK. An avenue of herringbone brick leads me past Poundland, Shoe Zone, Vodafone, Costa, JD Sports and Boots to the Morrisons car park which has been designed as a continuation of the shopping court, with the same style of brick flooring and antiquated lamps.

At the end of a covered walkway running along the front of Argos is the window of the Morrisons cafe, called Market Street Café. Inside, a few elderly people and parents with children drink milky coffee and eat baked beans. Morrisons likes to brand their stores as traditional covered markets, in which the fishmonger and butcher say 'hello' and trim your cuts to order. In a similar bid for authenticity, Tesco invents farm names for the packaging of their products, like Boswell Farms diced beef, Rosedene Farms blueberries and Willow Farm chicken. Fictional businesses from a fictional rural Britain.

It's outrageous, really, our exploitation at the hands of corporate entities, but people are so inured to marketing that they willingly comply, even at their own expense. I'm not exempt. I might be walking around superstores with my entitled sense of writer's detachment, but perhaps my behaviour is really an expression of love for the commercial landscape born from years of conditioning. Stockholm syndrome masquerading as critique. *How to Love Abattoirs* by Barry Cow. *Coop Life* by Hilary Hen. *Under the Patio* by Murdered Husband. *Car Park Life* by me. I don't know, but I feel suddenly bored of it all, tapping notes into my Samsung, a woman staring at me from behind the window with her mug of tea and cheese toastie. I'm bored of the architecture of consumerism. Bored of supermarket car parks. Bored of myself going on about it. I might even be wrong, too, in my assertation that they're inherently idiosyncratic. Maybe it's just my imagination and they really are all the same. After all, what's going to happen next today in this Morrisons car park? I expect I'll walk around and take photos of security cameras, wonky bollards and randomly placed shopping trolleys, perhaps an amusingly random piece of litter in a shrub. Maybe a Red Bull can or a child's sock or a condom. I'll observe someone being odd, either in their car or going to their car, or hanging around the perimeter. Then that will be that. Dear God. Sometimes I wonder if I've taken a wrong turning in life. I'm not really sure why I'm in Caerphilly looking around a superstore instead of wandering around the magnificent thirteenth-century castle or simply getting into my car and driving home to Hastings. If it's a cry for help, then it's a very long-winded one.

It's at this point of utter deflation that I notice an odd structure opposite the sliding doors of the Morrisons. It's a big green cage, around eight or nine feet tall, completely empty. It cannot be for trolleys because there's a designated trolley area to the other side of the doors which is in full use. The cage is something I've never seen before. Who or what gets kept in there?

An elderly man in a fleece with his toddler grandchild is walking just ahead of me. He notices the cage too, and says to the child, 'Look, a cage.' I deduce that it must be new. A cage built in preparation for an imminent imprisonment. I glance across the car park at the castle, the eastern gatehouse of which was used as a prison in the sixteenth century, brain keening for a connection, but I keep it in check. *See what's in front of you, Gareth, don't go on yet another mental wild goose chase*.

Intrigued now, I move past the trolley stacks and turn the corner of the far flank of the supermarket, where I find black vertical marks on the wall, like claw marks, as if something has scrabbled desperately at the brickwork. Directly to the left, a chain dangles amidst more scuffs and scratches. Dirty liquid pools out from the wall – leaked water, piss, or maybe even blood. A piece of graffiti reads Mersh Serag. I puzzle over it a while. Then quickly google it on my phone to check it's not a Welsh name or some other language. Perhaps it's an anagram and I need to unscramble the code. Eventually I hit on something: Harm Egress.

Harm – to injure someone
Egress – the act of leaving a place, to step out of somewhere

The act of leaving this place will injure someone. Is that

what it means? If so, is it a threat or a prophesy? This is remarkable. A minute ago I was bored, and now I am under threat of violent death. Only several feet away is a fire escape door with a charred lock and another series of five black marks, as would be made by the bloody hand of a murder victim as they slid to the floor. This part of the car park is the exit to the road, walled in what looks to be old stone, a remaining feature of something that existed before Morrisons and Castle Court. Over a zebra crossing is another overflow car park with high walls, filthy with exhaust stains and also scarred by similar scorch marks to those on the supermarket.

What has been happening here?

An area of thick cotoneaster is bifurcated by a desire path, so sharply defined it could have been made with a machete, the path hardened by trampling and littered with pine needles from the trees above. I follow it, noticing the socks, tissues and scraps of torn duvet strewn about. A white shirt has been draped on the foliage, possibly when someone was ordered to strip naked in front of their murderer, or the result of frantic undressing by a horny couple before mutant rats gnawed them to death.

I turn behind the back wall of the car park into an area that's well concealed by trees and shrubs, where I find more clothing, mainly women's apparel. At the end of the beaten track there's a tree stump with almost a dozen women's shoes placed on the dead branches. Clearly the work of a psychotic killer, displaying their trophies in this torture garden in the lee of the ancient castle.

HARM EGRESS.
Try to leave and you may die.

I feel distinctly unsettled at the sight of the shoe tree, especially after the cage, the chains, the scorch marks and the discarded clothes. Disturbed I may be, my mind warped by researching endless tales of car park violence, but these things are really there. I've seen them and now I cannot unsee them. However much I tried to back out of this project when despairing by the Morrisons cafe five minutes earlier, there is no escape for me from *Car Park Life*. That's what the graffiti means. If I try to extricate myself, terrible things will happen.

It's a warning I fail to heed.

Part Two
Spaces

Chapter Thirteen

Hit the North

It is the last big trip I make with my wife and children. With hindsight, it might be a mistake to take them on a northern tour of superstore car parks, but it is too good an opportunity to miss. As a father of young daughters, with a house in the throes of renovation and almost daily work commitments, it is not easy to travel for research purposes. My first two books, *Marshland* and *The Stone Tide*, are based entirely on walks I took with my dog Hendrix at lunchtime and weekends, straying not more than a few miles from home. I cannot do this if I am to write about British car parks. I need to leave the south and head north, where memories may lie buried in the car parks of my past, like dead English kings. Besides, we can make it a holiday and visit family and friends in Scotland. Everybody will be happy with that. I am sure of it.

The first stop is my childhood home town of Glossop in Derbyshire. I don't remember any chain stores in the town, only a supermarket called Shopping Giant and an independent mini-market called Brightmores, where I worked one summer for pocket money when I was twelve. But I am not here to explore a retail car park. This is a stopping point to stretch our legs before we head into Manchester to seek out the Makro of my youth, a deviation down memory lane. I take my daughters to my former home, a 1960s semi-detached at the end of a close beside a field with the railway line for the local train from Manchester. I show them the oak tree I used to climb, amazed that it is still there, the touch of its bark taking me back in time. We cut through long grass to the tiny railway arch, where my friends and I huddled beneath dripping stone, listening to trains thunder overhead. On the other side is the scrapyard where my brother and I were never allowed to go – but did, of course – to seek corrugated iron panels that made great jumps for our bikes. Beyond that is the tall white chimney of the defunct Ferro Alloys and Metals Ltd, which I used to imagine was a space rocket.

My daughters are five and six years old. They are not yet of an age where they find my childhood of any interest, so the tour is soundtracked by the tantrum screams of my firstborn, to the point where I yell, 'I give up,' and order everyone into the car. It is only later that I realise she is doing me a favour. Whenever I slip into landscape nostalgia, the lie of the halcyon past, I should be assailed by an enraged child's cry, the primal scream of a being who lives only in the present and is absolutely bored of this wallowing self-congratulation for a history that never was. My nostalgia is further undermined when I get to Makro less than an hour later and discover a car park so alien to my memory of it that I realise the entire memory is a fiction, throwing into doubt many other recollections from my life. It's therefore a relief to stop for the night in Lancaster, an unfamiliar place to which I've never been, somewhere I can view with fresh eyes.

Early the next morning, I leave my family sleeping in the hotel and head on foot to a Sainsbury's I've spotted on Google Maps, positioned on the bend in the River Lune to the north of the city. There is an out-of-town Asda superstore, but I've rejected it in favour of something a little more historical and part of the social fabric. Besides, I fancy a quick tour of Lancaster, which looks gorgeous in the morning sun. Church spires and tall Georgian buildings compete for light in a dazzle of angles, reflections sharp against the orange sandstone, the shadowy streets below a hiss of cars in the first throes of the commuter rush hour. I pass Palatine Hall, a grand Georgian council office building, formerly a music hall and cinema, overlooking the Queen Victoria Memorial in Dalton Square, a bronze statue of the monarch on a pedestal of Portland stone, flanked by lions. Beneath the Queen is a plinth with bas reliefs depicting scientists, politicians, artists and clergymen of the era, including Thackery, Faraday, Irving, Watts and Florence Nightingale. The bronze has turned lurid green, the surrounding stone tarnished by fumes, Britain's glorified past decayed. All is not lost, however. As I approach the Sainsbury's it is apparent that the Victorian dream has been repurposed for the convenient purchase of foodstuffs, booze and sundries.

John James Sainsbury, born in 1844, founded the famous supermarket chain that bears his name, but this Lancaster Sainsbury's predates his inaugural grocery store by six years. A stone inscription tells me that the building dates from 1863 and was donated to the people of the city by Samuel Gregson, MP, the former Mayor. This is the site of Lancaster's first public baths. On opening day, bells rang out across the city as the High Sheriff and boys of the National School marched in a procession from the town hall through streets lined with bunting. When the baths closed down, the North Western Electricity Board occupied the building. A stone crest set into the peak of the building reads: *Nisi dominus frustra*. A quick Google search finds an approximate translation by historian Mary Beard as, 'Without the Lord, frustration,' a contraction of Psalm 127, 'Unless the Lord builds the house, those who build it labour in vain.' It indicates that this is God's anointed Sainsbury's, or if not anointed, then *approved*.

Back in 1978, the *Architect's Journal* reported that 'supermarkets in old towns have a nasty habit of standing out like sore thumbs[7]', pointing to the necessity of these businesses to take up a large space and to entice passing cars and walkers. To counter these criticisms, and get their development applications accepted, chains such as Sainsbury's, Morrisons and Tesco often choose to appropriate architecturally significant buildings when they develop within historical towns and cities. This repurposing can extend the life of beautiful buildings and protect them from demolition, but in some cases the only part that is protected is the frontage, while the rest of the building is newly constructed, a process known as facadism. This is what has occurred here. In the 1990s the original building was dismantled, the stones carefully categorised and numbered, then rebuilt as a supermarket with a car park enclosed within the grounds by long, high stone walls, a cobbled perimeter separating it from the public paving slabs. Arches within the walls are grilled with wrought iron, bearing Lancastrian roses in their centre. Ivy creeps around and through the rails from inside the car park, hinting at a garden paradise within.

A tree-lined entrance road, bordered by raised beds of rosemary, sweeps me towards iron entrance gates set in the wall, slung open in a welcoming fashion like

7   'A Window on Shopping', *Architect's Journal*, 9 Aug 1978, p.245

a nobleman's house on a day of celebration. On the hill beyond, Lancaster Castle appears to rise from the supermarket roof, a Union Jack flapping from its turrets, alongside the tower of the Priory Church of St Mary, golden brown beneath a blue sky. This view embeds the Sainsbury's into its deeper historical setting. There is a grandeur to the car park, from the high stone walls to the neatly constructed islands of shrubs, with bins made of concrete on triangular plinths. A flapping banner promises GREAT PRICES while another tells of an egg fried rice that can be ready in just two minutes and costs only fifty pence. I believe it, too. There's gravity to these offers, slung between pillars of northern sandstone, stained with the blood, sweat and tears of kings, queens, industrialists and bathers. Perhaps even some of the notable persons depicted on the monument in Dalton Square came to this site, clutching towels and hair soap. There are four empty packets of Sterling cigarettes by a bin, a brand I am not familiar with, but which sounds like it could have been smoked by a crowd of preppy young nobles after a bathing session.

I don't take the obvious route towards the store doors but turn a sharp right where oak trees shade the railings, beyond which I can hear rushing river water and traffic on the bridge. I head towards what looks like a bus shelter in the far corner, but is actually an outdoor smoking bay with an ashtray and a wooden bench. From the number of butts clustered in the ashtray, or tossed on the ground, it is well-used, which I find strange. To smoke here you would need to walk out to this part of the car park after shopping, then head back to your car afterwards. But why do that? Why not wait until you get home? Why not take a stroll around the walls or go and stand by the river? Why take the time to smoke here, inside the car park? Or perhaps the supermarket regulars enjoy a sense of history here in the gaze of the castle, church spires and clock towers. Perhaps this is a destination in its own right.

As I poke around the smoking area a Honda hatchback pulls up. Inside is a man in his late twenties, wearing glasses. He lowers them, peering at me intently, as if wondering whether to park here or go to one of the many other vacant spaces. After a long pause, he reverses slowly into a lot right next to the shelter. I pretend to check my phone, so that he can get out of the car and I can get on with my exploration without any further interaction, but he doesn't move. He sits there, staring dead ahead at the car park. It could be that he's waiting for me to leave as I wait for him to leave. Suddenly, I find myself in an unexplained relationship with a stranger, and a weirdly needy one at that. It feels as if we could stay like this forever, but I break the spell by moving along the verge by the wall, leaving him behind. I don't turn to see what he does next. Some things are better left a mystery.

Close to the store, there's a trolley enclosure, then a cobbled area leading through an arched iron entrance to a sumptuous green lawn, a micro-park within the car park. A pathway takes me down into an underpass. I emerge on the other side to find myself on the wide bend of the River Lune where the A6 separates from the city and curves away across the water towards nearby Morecambe. Turning to look behind me, I can see that the car park forms the wall of the riverbank, a footpath running along it towards a suspension footbridge and a terrace of converted Victorian warehouses. The low tide has exposed a swathe of black mud, in which a gigantic piece of driftwood looks like a lizard dragging itself from the ooze. Gulls swoop over hogweed in a cacophony of cries. This seems a world away from the car park, but that's the truth of the city exposed. We live on temporary plateaus laid upon ancient marshlands, forests and rivers. This spot beside Sainsbury's car park is a borderland between the built environment and its primeval origins.

When I return through the underpass to view the superstore from the opposite direction, I can see a newer extension of the building to the rear, with smooth pale brown slabs pressed against the old reassembled stonework. This is housing for students, known as Victoria Court. The name is a doffed cap to those who carved *Nisi dominus frustra* on the facade back in the 1860s, believing God was on their side and the Empire was forever, nine years before John James Sainsbury opened his first store and sparked a chain of events that would lead to me here in the sunshine, beside the trolley stacks, buzzing with a strange joy.

———————————

Having seen the road to Morecambe so close to Sainsbury's, and knowing that it's a very short drive from Lancaster, I cannot resist paying a visit. I hurry back to the car and hit the road, hoping that my wife and children aren't too bored back at the hotel. Morecambe is a faded seaside town, once known as Bradford-on-Sea for the number of holidaymakers from Yorkshire who took advantage of the Little North Western Railway connection. All I know of the town apart from that is that one of its most famous sons, John Eric Bartholomew, took his stage name from his birthplace to become Eric Morecambe; that it was where twenty-three exploited Chinese immigrant cockle-pickers died in 2004 when they were caught out by the tide; and that there's an enormous retail park between the railway station and the sea.

It's mid-morning by the time I enter Morecambe's Central Retail Park, the likes of Morrisons, DW Sport, Homebase and Next housed in a modern building of brick and steel. It isn't serviced by one car park, but by a complex of interconnected parking areas with single-lane roads with residential names like Holmore Way, Baycliffe Crescent and Kilnbank Avenue connecting islands of smaller premises, like Frankie & Benny's, Dominos and a closed Blockbuster Video. The network hinges on mini-roundabouts that have been pimped with quirky themed artworks consisting of granite blocks and bird sculptures: a metal cockerel standing guard; razorbills in dramatic action poses; a couple of gannets in a courtship dance above an illuminated direction arrow. The roads are tributaries of a dual carriageway called Central Drive, which leads towards the sea, its central crash barrier entwined with sculpted steel waves and effigies of seabirds diving for fish. They've put an extraordinary amount of effort into stylising the car park, and for good reason. People arriving by train have to pass through the retail park to get to the promenade, so the car park must show off the town and its heritage.

A walkway contains an artwork called *Flock of words* in which the flagstones are inscribed with bird-themed poetry by Robert Burns, John Milton, William Wordsworth and Edward Lear. The route is lined with concrete benches engraved with collective nouns: A BADELYING OF DUCKS, A CHARM OF GOLDFINCHES and A CLATTERING OF CHOUGHS. Across a faded zebra crossing is a skating ramp plastered in graffiti, to complete the street look, slightly compromised by signs telling people not to smoke near children. On the opposite side is 'Festival Market', a covered market building with a row of closed, shuttered shops: Pleasureland, Johnny's Fun Factory and Trawlers Fish and Chips. There's a car park in front of these shops, too. Everything here is a car park, or linked to one, all the way down to the Morrisons, outside which brightly painted, cartoonish puffins, ducks and pigeons perch on every bollard. In front of the supermarket is a Victorian building that was the original railway station, now a 'Fayre and Square' chain restaurant called The Platform, with an adjoining visitor centre and a KFC.

The station must once have been a breathtaking entry point to the town. Travellers would have stepped through the doors to see the promenade in front of them, the mudflats stretching to a wide horizon, gulls wheeling in the sky. Of course, the sandflats are notoriously dangerous. Posters on walls warn that if quicksand doesn't get you, then the tide will. It's a more serious message than the one expressed by the cartoon birds and pretty poetry of the car park. The Central Retail Park wants to distract you from such deathly thoughts. It wants to ease the visitor in. It might be a consumerist shopping hub with soulless chain stores that can be found in any retail park across Britain, but it yearns to entertain, to say something about the coast, to enlighten and educate the visitor. It is by far the quirkiest retail park I have visited, but for sheer bravado, it's hard to beat the car park that I visit later that day, fifty miles to the north.

Chapter Fourteen

Space is the Place

There is so much to say about Sainsbury's in Penrith, it's hard to know where to begin, or how to order my thoughts. Whereas Lancaster's Sainsbury's was a reconstruction of a previous building on a site of significance, repurposing old materials, the Sainsbury's in Penrith uses new materials to build a faux-Victorian landscape and create a new site of significance imbued with all the implied authority of nineteenth-century architecture.

The Sainsbury's is housed in a grand sandstone building with a pediment and entablature above a series of columns with art deco tinted windows, and steps leading to a brick walkway. It looks like an old town hall. This harking back to the past began to characterise the architecture of superstores after 1978, when an Asda in Essex was designed with a pitched roof, gables and a clock tower, a style which became known as the Essex Barn and was widely adopted in the 1980s. The intention was to create superstores that were more sympathetic with the landscape, but also to brand them as authentic purveyors of wholesome, natural produce. Neo-modernist structures of glass and steel emerged in the mid-nineties, but never quite killed off the retro look, which evolved from the rural-inspired Essex Barn into the more urban, civic version here in Penrith. I understand why. In this country we prefer to dwell among facsimiles and facades, reassured by the convenient lie of the past, than to enter the future on new terms, with fresh ideas and a willingness to embrace change.

Standing sentinel outside the columned walkway, retro street lamps overlook the front car park, called 'Common Garden Square'. Instead of tarmac, cars drive over tessellated ochre brick, with contrasting dark grey bricks to demark the parking area, and pale grey to demark each lot. There is no white paint here. No scruffy symbols denoting parent-and-child parking. The wheelchair motif for disabled parking is formed from yellow brick, while even the zebra crossing is made from a mosaic of black and white bricks: a Lego version of reality. Overlooking a lush lawn, starred with daisies, is a monolithic slab of tourist information on a stone plinth. It says EDEN RIVERS, showing a network of local waterways, with bronze markers indicating locations of interest. On the other side is a history of Penrith with text and photographs.

Common Garden Square is the outward public face of the store. An adjoining section of the building to the left is more contemporary in style, tall yellow, red and brown metallic blades concealing a concrete double-decker car park, with ivy growing through metal mesh fences. I feel an embarrassing frisson of excitement, for this means that here are three car park types in one store – outside, covered and rooftop. A full house.

In the covered area, I am back to the conventional flooring of dark tarmac, with white and yellow painted lines. This bit knows it's a car park, but there is still something unusual. On each of the white pillars holding up the roof are squiggly geometric markings in the paintwork. The first is formed of two Ds facing apart, like fat blokes in a duel. The next is a zigzag, like a diagram of a stock market crash. Another looks like a domino and another looks like a tadpole race in a three-lane swimming pool, neighboured by a pattern resembling a swirling time tunnel from a 1960s science fiction television series. One pillar combines all the elements of its predecessors – the tadpoles, the parallel lines, the zigzags, spirals and D shapes – with the addition of smiley curves.

But is it accident or art? Are these the songlines of Sainsbury's?

The voice of a TV historian drifts into my head.

'Nobody knows anything about the humans who made these markings in a Cumbrian supermarket car park, but the evidence suggests that they were deeply spiritual, animistic and attuned to the local landscape.'

In the mid-twentieth century, English artist Brion Gysin created a series of calligraphic abstractions based on Japanese and Arabic scripts, which look remarkably like these patterns. He did it by carving a grid pattern into a wallpaper roller, then running it over canvas to scar and tear the material. A detail from one called *Magic Mushrooms* (1961) could have been displayed on a pillar in this Sainsbury's and I would not have noticed the difference. Gysin later evolved this idea of cutting random shapes and repeating them, but on a spinning metal cylinder with a light inside it. This was called the 'dream machine'. The aim was to flicker the light at a frequency of eight to thirteen pulses per second, corresponding to alpha waves in the human brain, putting the viewer into a hypnotic state. Perhaps this is why I find these calligraphic abstractions on the car park pillars so alluring. I assume that they are remnants of an adhesive which glued something to the pillars, but they're so varied you'd think there would be more consistency to the design, a singular gluing technique or application strategy, unless each one was performed by a different individual with a unique signature. The superstore opened in 2011, and it has only ever been a Sainsbury's, in which case what could have been attached to the pillars which needed to be removed? What sign became so swiftly redundant?

I begin to collect up all the artworks, moving between the cars, snapping them with my phone's camera, getting odd looks from shoppers. I catch the eye of the trolley attendant who isn't impressed, but equally isn't bothered. I lower the phone and follow the wall to the rear pedestrian exit, hung with vertical metal girders of yellow, beige, brown and pink. A mesh fence is bolted to the outside of the structure, forming a narrow, uncovered alleyway with no apparent purpose. On the other side of this mesh is a bank of wood chippings, monkey puzzle trees, conifers and pines, with bird feeding boxes attached to the trunks. The contrast of the variegated greens on one side of the fence and the stark grey concrete of the car park on the other forms a split-screen effect. It's a perfect representation of the anthropocentric concept of 'nature', in which nature is a thing separate from us, and that as long as we keep it nice *over there*, we can do what we like *over here*. We might build, destroy, pollute and consume but everything will be okay if we plant a forest to offset our actions, as if it is possible to balance the books, and we aren't ourselves nature, biological components of the earth, reaping the cost of our actions. Perhaps my obsession with the hieroglyphs on the pillars is an expression of a yearning to see something wild in concrete, the animism of artificial objects, spirits clawing for recognition and release.

I walk up a twisting ramp to the rooftop car park, which is completely empty like a mini airport runway. The green hills of the Lake District rise in the distance. Below the parapet I can look down at Common Garden Square, otherwise known as *the car park*. From this lofty vantage point I can see clearly now what is going on. The car park has a triple function: firstly, as a place to park your car; secondly, as a pretty place to sit on the grass, look at maps, get cash and wait for taxis; thirdly, as a gateway to Penrith. At the corner of Common Garden Square, to one side of the superstore, an overhead sign says 'New Squares'. From here, the car park segues into a walkway that meanders through a pseudo-village high street with higgledy-piggledy twists and turns. This brand new commercial zone, integrated into Penrith New Squares, was opened in 2013, but most of the shops are empty, with *Units Reserved* or *To Let* stickers on the glass. I take a photo of one of them and see the reflection of myself photographing me back.

At the end of the walkway there's what appears to be the back wall of an original Penrith building, overlooking an ornamental garden named Two Lions Square. Here is where the new and old join up. The online marketing blurb says: 'New Squares has been designed to extend Penrith town centre and complement the traditional architecture that makes Penrith so aesthetically appealing whilst providing modern shop units suiting the requirements of today's retailers.' To enjoy the shopping, you must access it through the gateway of the Sainsbury's car park, a facsimile of a public square, with gardens and a supermarket disguised as a town hall. The car park is also the destination. Space is the place.

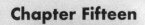

Chapter Fifteen
The Castle in the Car Park

During our trip north, I get a text message from Dan, my friend and co-walker in Plymouth's Crownhill Retail Park. He tells me that I absolutely must stop at Cairn Lodge services on the M74 and take a look around.

ME: *Cool thanks though not writing about service stations.*
DAN: *Yes but there's a castle in the car park!*

A castle in the car park? Sod the manifesto, this has to be worth a stop. I resist any attempt to research the castle, leaving only a mental note to stop. Hours of solid driving after the corporate magnificence of Penrith New Squares, we approach Crawford on the M74 as my daughters declare that they need the toilet, pleas that I ignore as the Abington Services Welcome Break sign appears, and which I continue to ignore as the Abington Services disappears behind us. 'Only a little further,' I say, pushing on the accelerator, aware that this is precisely the behaviour exhibited by my dad during long drives when I was a child.

Tensions are high and torrential rain begins to pour as we pull into Cairn Lodge. My wife remains in the passenger seat, jabbing at her smartphone as I usher the girls into the modest, one-storey building that houses a cafe, restaurant and shop. I cannot yet see a castle, but I wait patiently for them to emerge from the toilet then hurry them back into the car, where we wait for the deluge to subside a little.

'Let's all go and find the castle!' I say after a few minutes, to absolutely zero response from the back seat.

'Can we not?' says Emily.

'Girls?' I twist around to appeal to them.

'When are we getting to Scotland?'

'This is Scotland.'

'Oh.'

'Where else would you find a castle in the car park?'

They shrug.

'Okay, then stay here and I'll be back in a few minutes.'

I slam the door behind me and grab an umbrella out of the boot. There is no obvious sign for a castle, but a lack of sign doesn't mean a lack of the thing which is not signified. Besides, castles are not structures that can be easily missed nor mistaken for something else. I scurry down a promising pavement at the side of the restaurant building, where – I would say 'to my surprise', but Dan has already told me about it – I behold a small castle, pale brown against dark cloud, at the end of a paved walkway lined with picnic benches leading from the glass back doors of the services.

The castle consists of a gated arch within a crenelated tower, with walls on either side, bracketed by trees. The gate is locked and nobody else is out here. I stand for a few moments looking at it. I take a picture, then move closer and take another. I move to the side and take another at a slightly different angle. I can't think what else to do, or what further action to take. I could write something down, except I already have 'there is a castle in the car park' written in my phone notes. I add the colour of the car park: brownish grey. The size: small. The background: trees (don't know what kind, will show someone more knowledgeable a photo later). But then I struggle. I don't know whether it's the rain or the simmering resentment back in the car, but I feel paralysed by the weight of expectation, heavy as a thundercloud. Yes, there's a castle in the car park, but there's nothing I can do about this, except to acknowledge it. After all, the castle in the car park is just a castle in a car park. I have nothing more to ponder about this, other than the fact that it's there.

I'm reminded of the poem 'The Red Wheelbarrow' by William Carlos Williams:

> So much depends
> upon
>
> a red wheel
> barrow
>
> glazed with rain
> water
>
> beside the white
> chickens'

The poem is a riddle that cannot be explained by its parts and doesn't require a solution. It exists on its own terms. Irreducible. The image is the thing. It simply *is*. I wrote an essay on the poem in an exam for my degree in English Literature, about how the poem was aiming to become an object in itself, an artefact, timeless and pure. 'No ideas but in things,' as Williams once wrote. However, the main reason I chose to study the poem for the exam was that I could write many pages about modernist theories while only having to remember that one tiny poem, instead of memorising something complex like Eliot's *The Waste Land*. Laziness, really. All about passing tests rather than understanding more about the world. Yet here I stand, before a castle in the car park, with 'The Red Wheelbarrow' taking shape before me.

> so much depends
> upon
>
> a castle in the car
> park
>
> glazed with rain
> water
>
> beside the green
> trees

So much depends upon what I think about car parks. But do I really need to find out why there's a castle here, or interpret the meaning of such a thing? You may urgently wish to know why there's a castle in Cairn Lodge car park, but I don't know and it will most likely be on Wikipedia. All I can say is that my wife and kids are in the car while I'm under an umbrella staring at a castle in a car park, struck, suddenly, by the futility of it all. What is the point of all this writing? What good does this do? Why can't I just let things be?

I decide I can do nothing else but turn away from the castle in the car park and return to the car.

'How was it?' Emily asks, not in the slightest bit interested.

'It was a castle,' I say, 'in the car park.'

This is the last we ever speak of it.

Chapter Sixteen

Grave Business

After the strains of the northbound tour, we rest a few days in Glenlyon, in the Scottish Highlands, where old friends of mine run a croft, with chickens, pigs and polytunnels full of vegetables. Behind their garden, water the colour of whisky tumbles over a waterfall and cuts though a field of sheep beneath a hillside fuzzy with Scots pines. For many years, before marriage and children, this was my bolthole from London. Now I watch my daughters gambolling beneath trees while we drink wine and eat and talk. I don't mention the car park thing, as nobody is interested, but I'm painfully aware that my next stop is St Andrews, on the coast of Fife, where I spent my postgraduate year. The town is a key location in my as yet unfinished book *The Stone Tide*, in which my occult investigations of Hastings fuse with memories of my friend Mike's death in St Andrews two decades earlier, when he fell from the castle after a drinking session. I was the last person to see him alive beside the battlements on a drizzly night in May. I have not returned since a few years after the events described in my book, and the idea makes me nervous, but I feel I must do it. Nostalgia, perhaps, or this thing people call 'closure'. More likely it is so I can check how poorly I described the place from memory in my first draft and get it fixed for the second. Then afterwards, I can check out the town's superstore car park, if there is such a thing, for this altogether different kind of book, which I am determined not to turn into a tragedy.

I don't recall much supermarket shopping during my year in St Andrews, only pints of heavy in dark pubs, drunken walks down cobbled streets, icy sea swims and noisy living rooms full of cigarette smoke. I owned a car with which I could have driven to a superstore, but it usually sat empty of petrol outside the house. During a cold winter, the window was smashed and snow lined the back seat, and it remained that way a while. I see it in my mind's eye now, standing with my children at the same spot on a warm summer day, staring up at our old house. Directly opposite is St Andrews Castle, innocuous in the sun, busy with ambling tourists, chirpy voices and laughter.

I pay for a family ticket to enter the castle, which is something I've never done before. In 1996, we'd wait until the pubs closed then leap over the railings with a bottle of whisky and use the castle grounds as our playground for the night, listening to the sea crash against the rocks below or, like Mike, climb up the walls. At the same slab of medieval stone where I saw him last I feel I can reach out and touch the past, return to that fateful moment, as if the decades had never passed. It's how I felt caressing the bark of that oak tree in Glossop beside my childhood home. I don't know why it surprises me that some things stay the same or, at least, decay more slowly than me. It's odd, the sadness I feel at the persistence of places from my past, the weight of them on my soul, their very existence in the world. It's as if I prefer them to roar into flames behind me, leaving only scorched earth, no traces. Despite this, I persist in writing about that past, even when I'm not sure of its truth, so that it pervades all my fictions and non-fictions – even this book about retail store car parks. I cannot pull myself free from the glue of time, as I am trying to do now in the fateful grounds of St Andrews Castle. The tourists milling around me are happily exploring a fourteenth-century ruin, but all I see is the scene of a tragedy in 1996, and all I feel is the sadness of its aftermath.

I need to leave.

We drive south on the A915 to the Morrisons at the edge of town. I have no idea if there was a supermarket on this site when I did my masters' degree. If there was, I can't remember coming here. This part of St Andrews is at the periphery of my experience, a location in my past to which I might not have been. I park on the road beside some swollen topiary, hiding the lawns of pebble-dash houses. Leaving the family engrossed in their phones and tablets, I walk down the access road, the verge of a blaze of yellow flowers on cinquefoil. A tree with its bark shorn is surrounded by coppiced stumps and the first green shoots of the aftermath. A banner above a bed of purple and white flowers contains photos of giant beef burgers and declares that *Summer's here*. Rising from the lush green shrubs, a sign declares: *Customer only car park, for use only whilst shopping on the site. 2 hour max stay*. Beyond a fallen concrete post is a wall concealing the delivery truck yard, with this text bolted onto the steel fence above it:

Please work quietly...
Drivers must:
switch off engines and refrigeration motors
when stationary.

All staff:
No shouting
Keep noise to a minimum
Please respect our neighbours

Another declaration tells leafleteers that this is not a public right of way. Usage of the car park is *restricted to short stay shoppers only and proceedings will be taken against those entering into this development for any other purpose.* Because I am not here to park or shop, they could have legal recourse against me. This space may look flowery and inviting, but its aim is to get you to shop for as long as possible and then leave quickly. It is not a park. I read another sign which lays out legal rights and processes, with a glossary of what the markings on the tarmac mean: disabled, parent-and-child, yellow 'no parking', with a fine of £85 for failure to comply. Another tells me that *CCTV is in operation.* Yet another sign details the anatomies of the various Morrisons shopping trolleys, modifications and attachments:

Shopping trolleys
Daily shopper
Baby Cradle/Child Seat (only one baby, up to
9kg – child up to 15kg)
Twin Child Seat
Portable Baby/Child Seat
Family Trolley
Wheelchair Trolley

Even the trolley bays in this car park are insistent, with signs plastered on both sides and at both ends: PLEASE COLLECT AND RETURN YOUR TROLLEYS HERE THANK YOU. To soften the shouty ALL CAPS, the lettering is in a funky font, reversed out. It's in stark contrast to the italicised handwriting style of '*See you later*' by the pedestrian exit. This car park struggles to hit the right balance in tone between stern legalese and a sense of fun, between duty and love, like a conflicted Victorian father.

Unlike most Morrisons I've investigated, ashtray bins and benches have been placed throughout the car park, not only outside the main door. The implication is that they don't mind you hanging around for a while, as long as you're not doing one of the things on the extensive banned lists bolted to the wall, and you've bought shopping, and you're not annoying the neighbours. In other words, *sit down, shut up, don't do anything, and enjoy yourself*. That's not an order, of course, it's simply very strong advice, backed up with legal implications if you don't comply.

In one of the bench-side ashtrays all the butts have been pushed into one half of the sandy circle, as if deliberately arranged that way. And why not? This activity is not banned under any of the declared rules. This is one of the things you *can* do, a small act of expression from someone who sat on this bench and thought, *To hell with it, I am going to create a half-moon of filters*. I feel a twinge of pride at humanity's urge for artistic expression even in repressed conditions. This Morrisons ashtray is like a work by my favourite Russian writer, Daniil Kharms, who wrote absurd prose miniatures in the 1930s called 'incidents', plots stripped to the bare bones in order to avoid censorship and harassment. One of his stories goes like this:

> On one occasion a man went off to work and on the way he met another man who, having bought a loaf of Polish bread, was going his way home.
>
> And that's just about all there is to it.

It reads like a Stalinist version of *Car Park Life*. I take a photo of the ashtray with the intention of getting it enlarged and framed for my living room, then continue towards the edge of the car park, which overlooks another car park, that of the St Andrews Community Hospital. It looks remarkably similar to the supermarket car park. There is a Lloyds pharmacy in it, a private business, whereas in this Morrisons there is a pharmacy offering free NHS services and 'healthy lifestyle management' advice. A sign says: *NHS Fife has entered into a contract with Wm Morrison Pharmacy to dispense drugs.* As an increasingly privatised NHS begins to charge for healthcare, the supermarkets will offer services for free, not for philanthropic reasons but to attain and retain custom. There is a mission creep on both sides, from public sector to private, from private to public, with the superstore assuming a paternal role. For instance, the 'do your bit' sign on the window urging the customer to recycle – a typical transferal of responsibility for pollution to individuals by the corporations who cause the mess in the first place. *You got the bags made and packaged everything in plastic in the first place, you bastards.* I resent the finger-wagging of supermarkets that tell you to follow their instructions, give them your money, then feel guilty for your behaviour. It's the same as the charity mega-events on TV that want the poorest in society to pay for welfare which the government should offer. Let the masses fish for shrapnel in the sofa while politicians profit from property empires and business consultancy earnings. *DO YOUR BIT for the environment,* says Richard Branson, owner of an airline. *DO YOUR BIT SO I CAN KEEP MAKING MONEY.*

I'm irritated, suddenly, but in that same instant I realise that my thoughts have nothing to do with Mike, or my time in St Andrews. He's not here. That past is not here. Instead, these familiar frustrations tell me that I'm in car park world, a space with its own politics, culture and memory. Not an unplace, but a place apart. Perhaps this is why I'm drawn to it. It's a form of self-exile. A way to distract myself from my compulsive nostalgia, all that guilt and regret, wandering a landscape that few care about, where the people are many, yet anonymous, and in which nothing much happens, yet almost anything can.

On the way to Edinburgh we stop at the ring road cemetery where Mike is buried, a place I've not visited since the funeral. Emily waits in the car with the girls, just like they do at the car parks, except now I feel acutely lonely, their stares burning into my back as I walk into a territory of which I have little recollection.

Mike's sister has given me rough directions to where he is buried, but it's hard to distinguish because everything looks the same – bright green lawn within well-trimmed hedgerows, dotted with conifers, a road lined with benches cutting through. It's not much different to the Morrisons car park, except each lot is filled with dead bodies. I reach the zone in which Mike is buried but I don't know which row he's on, and there are at least twenty to choose from, so I walk up and down each one, reading the engravings. On the day of the funeral there was no headstone, only a hole in the ground, so when I find it I'm surprised to see that it says *Michael*, when in my head it said *Mike*, and the stone is smaller than I expected, a marble plaque next to that of a woman of a similar age, which pleases me for no rational reason. After all, the dead don't date.

As I kneel and say, 'Hi Mike,' I try to remove the image from my head of a corpse beneath my feet. 'So here you are. Long time no see.' Stupid thing to say, not that he cares. After a few seconds I stand again, wondering what to do next. I have never visited a grave before. All my deceased family members have been cremated and flung to the winds. I'm struck by the horticultural beauty of Mike's surroundings, the plants and shrubs, tall trees and rockeries. Cemeteries used to be in the centres of towns and villages, but gravitated out towards the ring roads. Relatively few people come here each day, but enormous attention is spent on how the landscape will make them feel – calm, reflective, peaceful. On the contrary, supermarket car parks are hubs of daily life, where people visit regularly, but they don't get the same care and attention. It seems the wrong way around. The dead live in luxurious gardens, while the living scrabble around on slabs of tarmac, awash with oil and rain.

Of course, not all the dead are left to rest in peace for long. Car parks are sometimes built on cemeteries. The Aldi car park in Stalybridge, Greater Manchester, is built on the burial ground of a Methodist chapel. In 2017, contractors were digging when they discovered a human skull and shoulder blade. Police were called in to check if the remains were recent, though its likely these were the bones of a once-loved person, whose family wept as they were lowered into the grave, a stone marker placed above them with a sense of finality. But time wears down the stone as quickly as it does the memory of that person – mother, grandmother, great-grandmother, great-great-grandmother, great-great-great-grandmother – gone. Few remember. Few care. The church is demolished. The stones are moved. The cemetery becomes parkland, then that parkland is turned into a car park as pressure for urban space builds. And so your great-great-great-great-great-grandmother ends up buried beneath Aldi, God rest her soul.

The Asda in Crawley, West Sussex, is built on the site of the demolished St Andrew's Presbyterian Church. Local rumours abound that a notorious serial killer is buried there, and that his ghost haunts the car park. People report flickering lights, guttural howls, floating groceries and eerie drops in temperature. 'There is something weird going on,' an Asda staff member told the *Daily Star* in 2010, revealing that the manager once asked a pagan priest to come and exorcise the evil presence.

Weird events transpired in York in 2011, when drivers filling up with fuel at the Clifton Moor Tesco forecourt could not start their cars when they tried to drive away. Others returned from the shop to find themselves locked out. A Tesco spokesperson told the media that they were baffled by this 'mysterious force' but suggested that it might be related to the electronics that control the pumps. This is a typically secular reaction by supermarket management suits. While there is no evidence that the Clifton Moor Tesco is built on a burial ground, York is one of Britain's most haunted cities and the supermarket location is not far from the River Ouse. It is said that waterways are natural conduits for spirits, so there is the possibility that the Clifton Moor Tesco filling station forecourt has been leaching some of that aquatic energy, or become the focus of eco-aware ghosts, furious about anthropogenic global warming, railing against our fatal addiction to petroleum, switching off car engines as a warning to us all.

Admittedly, there is not an abundance of haunted retail spaces in Britain. But if ghosts exist, there's no reason why they shouldn't haunt Aldi or Asda. We spend much of our lives in car parks, and very little in cemeteries, so I don't expect Mike's ghost lingers where he is buried. It's not a place he would recognise. He would be back at the castle in St Andrews, most likely, or up one of his beloved French mountains, or sat in the pub, guffawing. However, if I were to return as a ghost, my bizarre habit of wandering car parks might have an influence on my afterlife behaviour. The phantom Gareth E. Rees might be glimpsed drifting through retail zones, warning terrified shoppers about the folly of rampant consumerism while sneaking a judgmental peek at the food in their trolleys and tutting most spectrally.

Chapter Seventeen

Dockland

ASDA

part of the WAL★MART family

24 hours

Café

Lottery

Click & Collect

Click & Collect

George.

Leith lies to the north-east of Edinburgh, on the Firth of Forth. Its Premier Inn is right on the waterfront. From the window of our ground-floor room we can see boats crossing the estuary beneath a red evening sky. It's a premier view. The area around us is a peninsula of regenerated dockland, with glamorous apartment blocks along the shore with names like The Breakwater Apartments, Grand Harbour Apartments, Edinburgh Waterfront Apartments and The City Suites, surrounded by scrubland and concrete. It's like Scotland trying to be Dubai but looking like the Costa Brava in the 1980s. A bid for glamour in an industrial landscape, stalled in the aftermath of the 2008 financial crash. Wipe out. Surf's up. The spray hits the *To Let* signs on empty apartment windows.

Premier Inn is my favourite budget hotel chain. There's something reassuring in its bland uniformity, the purple fabrics, the extra pillows, the cutesy sleeping moon signage, the knowledge that nobody is watching you nor cares about you. They're the opposite of guest houses, which I loathe. The omnipresent owners reminding you that this is their house, with their rules. The judgmental look when you ask for beans instead of tomatoes. The idiosyncratic decor, trinkets and artworks, suggesting details of lives you don't want to know about – Margot and David's travel souvenirs and a shit watercolour by their niece who's in Australia now, as they told you minutes after you arrived and then again at breakfast where they made you sit at a shared table with other mortified guests. I'd take a Premier Inn any time. Devoid of individuality, it's a safe space where you don't feel beholden, nor under scrutiny. When you leave you can drop your key card though the slot without saying goodbye. They don't mind. It's what they want. Minimal contact means minimal friction means minimal costs for both them and you. It's the perfect low maintenance relationship. No strings. No commitment. No guilt. Premier Inn is my hotel fuck buddy.

It's early morning and I'm outside the main door, beside the purple branded Premier Inn flowerpots. It has been raining and the tarmac is damp, puddles shimmering. Ventilation fans whir beyond the fence of the Brewers Fayre as pigeons scrabble from beneath roof slats to peck around some wooden tables scattered with tomato ketchup sachets, cigarette butts and Costa coffee cups. A gull has attacked a bin and left a trail of smashed eggshells. In the al fresco dining area, the closed red umbrellas are like Imperial Guards from the *Star Wars* films. Beds full of spiky yucca plants look tropical against the blue sky and the white lighthouse.

I walk down the side of the hotel to the harbour wall, moored boats bobbing, where a man with a dog gestures frantically at an aggressive gull and my nose fills with salty ozone from exposed rocks. The rear of the Premier Inn is at the top of a cobbled slope that slants into the waves of the Forth of Firth. I remain here a while, soaking it in, before heading back across the lawn, a Jessie J song blasting from an empty tour coach.

At the other side of the peninsula, only five minutes' walk away, is Leith's Asda superstore, my destination for the morning, and the final car park of this trip. I head towards the silhouettes of dock cranes and a ship moored beneath a monolithic rectangular industrial building joined to another by a diagonal walkway in the sky. Below is Asda, a contemporary steel and glass structure, outside which boat sails advertise Scottish Hydro Electric. The car park is bordered with stone slabs and trees in square enclosures, while its entrance walkway is covered in the same domed Perspex roofing as the trolley bays, so it looks like I am entering a trolley-bay-themed wedding marquee. The trolley guy is only just wheeling the stacks into place for the first customers of the day. There is nobody here but two large bald men in tracksuits, intently studying a stack of plastic garden furniture.

In the same way that St Andrews' Morrisons is keen to adopt the mantle of local community service hub, this Asda offers a 'free glasses MOT', cleaning services, twenty-four-hour cash, automatic fuel pumps, and even an NHS Scottish Breast Screening Programme, hosted in a prefab in the car park. In a framed poster for Asda Money, a giant hand waves a wad of euros. Wherever you're going, you'll get good rates in store, it tells me. Supermarkets can look after your eyes, sort your finances, screen you for cancer, feed you and fill your car with petrol. What more do you want (apart from happiness, hope and freedom from pain)? There's even a recycling enclosure behind tall wooden slats adorned with the phrase 'Always happy to help'. I can hear the high-pressure hiss from the truck washing facility in front of the industrial building looming above me as I walk down an tarmacked path through a low-walled garden that feels like the car park, but I'm not sure if it is, for it has no function other than a place for dwelling by the edge of the quay, where the *Troms Hera* ship is moored, hull towering, upper decks bristling with aerials, held fast by ropes as thick as my arms, so close I can reach out and touch the yellow mooring bollard. It's as if the supermarket is luring visitors to the dockside to enjoy the spectacle, creating its own tourist viewing point so that they can get close to the ships and feel the spirit of Leith's industrial heritage. Asda wants you to see the docks through the prism of Asda, same as it wants you to see through Asda glasses and go on holiday with Asda euros. The ship is owned by Troms Offshore, who specialise in Platform Supply Vessels (PSV) for oil rigs. It looks freshly washed, moored at Asda for a brief respite before it is banished once more unto the cruel sea.

Asda is less keen for customers to enjoy the rubble wasteland behind the unmanned petrol pump at the back of the car park, where an earthwork and fence hide the view. A sign tied to the fence reads:

BEDROOM CEILING now painted as the TWINKLING NIGHT SKY.

It's an ad for a local business called Night Sky Cosmic Ceilings, whose website explains: 'Instead of looking up at a dark, blank space that is your normal ceiling you will now see your own Universe spread out before your eyes.' This feels familiar to me, a wanderer of car parks. I know the wonder of a bland space transformed with a little imagination. Beyond the bombast of the dockside, there is magic in the details of this Asda car park too, for as I return to the access road I notice that the verge is not made of the usual wood chippings or stones, but scallop shells, thousands and thousands of scallop shells, an infinite galaxy of the dead. A voice in the wind whispers, 'Oh my God! — It's full of stars!' My trip is over. I have travelled so far in such a short space. Now it is time to return to earth with an almighty crash.

Part Three
Exit

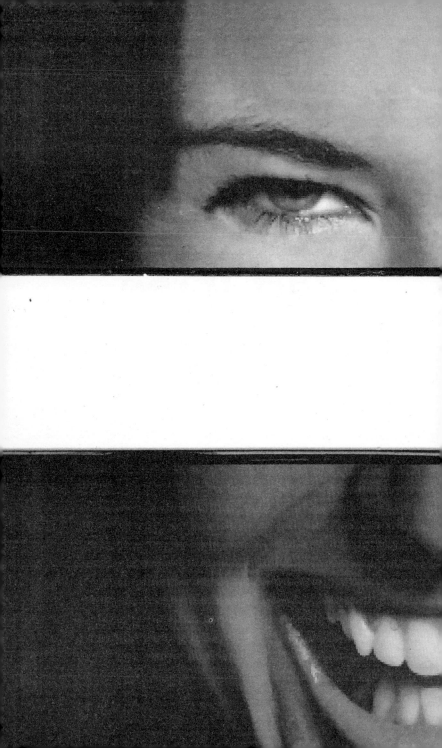

Chapter Twenty

Brexit

If someone had told me, on New Year's Eve 2015, that next year I would lose my marriage and my home, Britain would decide to leave the European Union, and a dangerously populist, racist tycoon would take charge of the United States, I'd have rolled my eyes and poured another cava. I'm a pessimist by nature but even that kind of prediction is too much. Yet it all comes to pass. In March, my marriage ends, and not by my choice. Within a couple of months of tumultuous revelations, leaving no chance of resolution, an assumed future disappears, like a photo in flames. Family Sunday lunches together, my wife and I, opening our presents at Christmas, watching school plays and concerts, celebrating anniversaries in cosy restaurants, welcoming our grown-up children home as grey-haired pensioners. It all vanishes. The events are such a shock that I have not speculated once about an alternative reality without my wife and family being together, or what that might look like. I don't know where I am going to live, how I am going to live, or what kind of father I am going to be to my children. I have no image of the future at all. There is nothing ahead but a white fog.

I am in a miserable state a few months later when I travel across Kent to the Whitstable Literary Festival, where I am booked to read at an event with my publishers, Gary Budden and Kit Caless. On impulse, I book a Premier Inn without thinking of the emotional connotations. Both the benefit and the curse of the hotel chain is its brand continuity. The purple fabrics, the plastic key cards, the sleepy moon sign, the spare pillows, the overpriced breakfast. They're the same wherever you go. In Whitstable, I feel like I am in all the other Premier Inns I have visited with my wife and kids, resonant with their voices, their bickering over the bed, the flicking through the channels for CBeebies, and I pine deeply for this close past which has been lost. A budget hotel I loved for its soulless functionality is now horribly resonant with memory, fills me with melancholy, and exists in almost every town and city in the country, like a branded chain of haunted houses. When what is convenient and familiar turns sour, it becomes a torment, not a sanctuary. Throwing myself onto the purple bed, alone, crushed by the weight of my failure, I feel like a divorced travelling salesman.

To make matters worse, not many people turn up to our event and we read to about ten attendees. It is an improvement on an event I did where three writers read to two people, one of whom left halfway through. Gary and Kit tell me they once held an event in Margate where they lost most of their attendees to a packed book signing down the road for Boycie from *Only Fools and Horses*. The indie literary scene is not for the thin-skinned, faint-hearted or profit-hungry. Afterwards we drink in The Old Neptune pub on the beach, where a Bob Dylan tribute band plays, then I walk in an inebriated daze back to the Premier Inn, claim my extra pillow from the wardrobe and fall asleep, half dressed, to late-night television.

Car Park Life

The next morning, I head down the coast to Reculver, a few miles east of Herne Bay, to walk on the crumbling sandstone cliffs. There's the ruin of a twelfth-century church on the site of a seventh-century monastery, itself on the site of a Roman fort, overlooking a beach strewn with late Palaeocene bivalve fossils, where they tested Barnes Wallis's bouncing bomb. To the west is the Isle of Sheppey, with a faint suggestion of Essex on the skyline. To the east, Margate sparkles in the sunshine. Out to sea, the rusted gun towers of the Maunsell Forts stand beyond rows of gleaming white wind turbines. There are so many histories visible from this one spot, it's dizzying. Stories of invasion and assimilation, adaptation and innovation, change and renewal, all laid out across this coastal stage. There are some Brexit voters who complain about a cultural erosion of Britain caused by immigration. At what arbitrary point in history would they like time frozen? What evidence is there in nature of the possibility of total stasis, never mind the benefits? Even rocks are slow life. Nothing remains the same. The past was never ideal and the future won't be either. *Que sera, sera.*

Standing in this vortex of epochs, the sea stretching to infinity, the catastrophe of my marriage break-up becomes momentarily shrunken, as if I can pick it up and examine it properly for the first time, even laugh at it, like Gulliver with a Lilliputian in his hand, then gently let it go. No wonder so many people come to this spot to unburden their grief. On a wire fence overlooking the cliff edge beside the church, I find dozens of tiny bunches of dried-up flowers with laminated memorial notes scrawled in splodgy fountain pen. On the beach below, shells pressed deliberately into the soft sandstone write out messages of love and RIPs. There are pyres of stones and nooks hacked into the cliff to burn fires. This is where the young and disaffected come to drink, get stoned and tell stories. I wonder why anyone would hang out in a car park after dark when there's a place like this, layered with history, widescreen in scope, surrounded by materials so malleable you can literally carve out your niche and write yourself into the landscape. Then again, most people in Britain don't live in places like this.

On the way home, I stop at Herne Bay, where I park in front of the Morrisons on the high street a few roads behind the promenade. Beneath navy roof tiles streaked with gull shit, giant images of limes harmonise with the stacks of green shopping trolleys and the white panels of the Click & Collect pickup point. It's the perfect car park to visit after the cliffs of Reculver, as its car park is up on the roof, a rare feature for a Morrisons. A vertical sign with CAR PARK and a direction arrow leads to a driveway beside Herne Bay Plant Hire, its yard stacked with silver ladders. Can this really be the way in? As I turn the corner, I see a concrete access ramp curve up to the roof, split by a bright yellow raised concrete strip running down its centre.

One lane says THIS WAY UP and the other says NO ENTRY. The old version of me would have transgressed by walking up the NO ENTRY lane. An up yours to the car park overlords. But the new me, undergoing marriage separation, chastened by a barely attended literary performance, holds no stock in those old pleasures. I need more. So I step onto the raised central strip, barely wide enough for both of my feet, and ascend like a tightrope walker. Perhaps I am the only person ever to do this. In this moment I am Captain Scott or Neil Armstrong. It is the stuff of dreams. I have wandered alone on a volcano in the middle of Lake Nicaragua; I have stood in the psychedelic plains of Patagonia, thumb out in the hope of a passing vehicle; I have walked through a smoking lava flow in Iceland; but here on the central barrier of the concrete access ramp to Herne Bay's rooftop Morrisons, I am a true pioneer, striding the untrammelled borderland between two directions. What is it even called, that which I am walking on? This nameless thing? This third way? This rib of light?

As the ramp curves back on itself towards the rooftop, I see a security camera aimed at me and I give it a wave. Ha ha! They can't see me in this liminal space. I am nowhere man!

Meanwhile, in the CCTV observation room...

DEREK: We've got another one.

JIM: Really? So soon?

DEREK: Uh-huh.

JIM: Going up the yellow barrier?

DEREK: Of course. They always go up the yellow barrier.

JIM: Gawd. What is it this time?

DEREK: Man in his forties. Scruffy looking.

JIM: Classic.

DEREK: Thinks he's Neil bloody Armstrong. Look at him.

JIM: Has he waved?

DEREK: Yep.

JIM: Wish we could stick all this stuff on YouTube.

DEREK: The idiot channel.

JIM: Maybe we should write a book about it.

DEREK: Waste of time, mate. Nobody wants to read about car parks.

At the top of the access ramp a hastily handwritten sign says, *Car park open as usual*, as if a terrible incident has recently occurred up here on the roof. I study the battered tarmac plateau. There are splatters of shiny black, leaked oil or the surface melting in the sun. Silver ventilation chimneys are dented. Inside a cage, generators rattle and cough. The white lines are faded, signs of hasty surface repair evinced by geometric blobs and strips. A steel guard rail runs along the wall, knee-high, with signs warning me not to stand on it, for there is a precipice on all sides. There aren't many supermarket car parks where you are constantly seconds from death. I feel that familiar compulsion to hurl myself off the edge, but I stand on the rail anyway. Down below I can see a construction site, possibly for a new chain store with a new car park. Cells divide and replicate. Organisms evolve. Life goes on, and on, and on, I tell myself, even when I come to an end. My marriage is over but something else will begin. My future was one thing, and now it's another.

A month later, what happened to my marriage happens to the whole of the UK, when the referendum goes in favour of leaving the EU. The morning after the vote I am sick with despair. I pass my wife coming down the stairs from the spare bedroom and she's shaking her head about the result too, which is almost funny, bearing in mind what is happening to our family, torn in two, awaiting physical separation when we finally sell the house. I cannot face working at home today. I crave some of the exhilaration I felt in Reculver. A landscape that might put the world into perspective. So I drive westward along the coast to Pevensey Castle, where I park up, don a pair of walking boots, then stride out onto the levels, a lowland of green and purple fields scattered with farmhouses, criss-crossed with drainage ditches. In Roman times, it was a lagoon that flooded at high tide. The Anglo-Saxons later exploited the marshland for salt making. Even when most of the land had been reclaimed from the sea, flooding remained a threat. There are several rumpled hillocks in the flatland which were once home to bustling medieval villages. Like Reculver, this is a layered landscape shaped and scarred by constant flux, but I don't feel the same uplift in my spirit today, only a sense of unbearable strain. The sun is a disc of pale fire behind cloud. Two swans fight in a lily-clogged water channel. Methane steams from cowpats. The sounds of the A27 and A259 blend with the clang of farm machinery and the agonised low of cattle from a distant shed. This compromised landscape struggles with itself. Dandelion spores trapped in thistles speak of aborted hopes. A buzz saw takes down a tree. I enter a field where a flock of sheep are running at pace, but there's no sign of a shepherd, nor a dog. Brexit panic among the log piles, pylons and telegraph poles. None of this is cheering me up. It is making things worse.

I walk down Rickney Lane, a B-road that weaves back towards Pevensey, lined with blackberry bushes, the first fruits of summer beginning to form. The reflector posts to help cars navigate tight corners at night are mostly smashed or toppled. As I progress, the amount of litter in the verges increases – chocolate eclair and sherbet straw packets, Quavers, plastic cups and Stella cans. There is usually litter at the sides of roads but this is intense, almost as if it has been left here for me, a Hansel and Gretel trail of detritus, leading me towards the witchy truth – and sure enough, there it is – a Marks & Spencer in the local services at the roundabout. I tried to escape into the countryside but ended up back in a car park. Perhaps escape is not possible for any of us, as we head for a political, economic and ecological cliff edge, driven by billionaire media moguls and right-wing ideologues who will sell off everything we hold dear in the name of protecting British culture. We get the landscapes we deserve and what we deserve is the chain store car park.

In weary acceptance of my fate, I drive to the massive Asda superstore near Pevensey Bay where I stroll through its car park for half an hour, just for the hell of it, not even worrying about taking notes for this book. I am not sure if my head is still in the Pevensey Levels, but it seems like there is a lot of greenery, from the pine trees and dividing shrubs to the Asda logo to the trolley handles and *Save money live better* posters on the lamp posts. Commerce and nature sharing the colour of reassurance, but despite this I feel uneasy. The giant faces of the Asda models emblazoned on the windows of the building are hideously distorted by white PVC cross-beams. A young woman's head is split into two segments, nose and mouth in one, eyes and forehead in another. She grins maniacally, clawing at her temple, as if cognisant of her own mutation. Next to her, a blond boy with missing teeth appears to claw at the window, face stained by a mist of black residue. Then there's a toddler, head split into three squares, her fractured psyche emblazoned on the side of a supermarket as if this is completely normal. She appears to be shrieking for help.

Car Park Life

This Asda is of a neo-modernist design, with pitched glass roof supported by steel beams, and an atrium-style entrance. Viewed from the front, the building is shaped like an A. I assume A is for Asda. Architecture as branding. Or perhaps it is supposed to look like a church, the spire pointing to God. These contemporary supermarket designs attempt to move away from the traditional Essex Barn structures, but they still hark back to the past, their high glass roofs inspired by Victorian covered markets. Asda cannot escape from history, any more than the people of Britain seem able to, trapped in our dream of rural idylls and lost empires.

That winter, Donald Trump is elected to the office of President of the USA on the back of promises to Make America Great Again. Life isn't just changing dramatically for me, but for the whole world. My wife and I finally sell our house and split-up. I move into a place on the West Hill above Morrisons in Hastings, the elevation I used to look up at from the car park. Only a few minutes' walk from my front door and I can see the supermarket splayed across the narrow valley below, glimmering in the darkness. The light from the M is broken, so it says 'orrisons'. I recall that night when I first walked drunkenly though its car park on the way home from the pub and saw its capacity for magic, mystery and revelation. Now it looks like it's falling apart.

On the final day of the year, I drive from my parents' house in Amesbury to Hastings for the New Year's Eve's celebrations. But as I exit the M3, I feel no real desire to celebrate, only to hibernate. I don't really want to go to Hastings, and neither do I wish to return to my parents' house. Halfway down the M25 I pull into Cobham services, where my wife and I would regularly meet my parents to hand over the girls when we needed a few days' babysitting, or someone to look after the dog. Cobham is an ideal rendezvous point, as it can be accessed from both directions of the motorway. I know it better than any other service station, a modern glass building offering curries, noodles, burritos, Marks & Spencer, Costa and a Days Inn chain hotel for the weary traveller.

I park up, but I don't get out of the car. I'm not hungry. I don't need a piss. I just need some time. A bit of stillness. I'm aware that I am now one of those people I keep seeing in my car park walks, sat alone in their vehicles, silent and staring. But I cannot see any reason to move. There is no point to anything. Nothing I do will make a difference to how I feel. Perhaps I should rent a room at the Days Inn and spend New Year's Eve in a service station on the M25, the road to nowhere. Nobody will miss me in Hastings and my parents will presume I am partying happily. In the Days Inn I can disappear. Fall through a crack. Exist between places, almost as if I am nowhere at all. But this notion also terrifies me. I am not the first emotionally distressed person to think like this. Many times I've opened the window of a chain hotel to find that a metal bar stops it moving more than a few inches, to prevent guests hurling themselves out. I don't feel suicidal, just an urge to switch off the engine and stop the ride, if only for a moment. However, it isn't a good idea to put this assumption to the test in a Days Inn on the M25. Instead, I will go to the pub in Hastings, get pissed, and everything will be fine. Of course, it won't be fine, we're all in really deep trouble, but after four pints I can convince myself of anything.

With a sigh I turn on the ignition and head towards an uncertain future.

Chapter Twenty-One

Dirty Bits

I'll make this crystal clear. The idea of chatting-up a stranger in a supermarket appals me. Small talk cannot happen at the meat counter. Nor can it occur beside the iced corpses of fish, beneath the crazed glare of the Honey Monster, in the toilet roll aisle, or anywhere near baked beans. There is no good place to stand and talk to anybody about anything in a supermarket, unless it's to ask an employee for the location of a food item. In the glare of strip lighting, romance is not on my mind. My loins are not stirred by the sound of clattering trolleys, wailing toddlers and elderly couples bickering over crisp flavours. The pop hits of yesteryear, crackling over the sound system, fill me with either teary nostalgia or blind rage, but never the urge to mutter something seductive to the woman buying a paella ready meal. What could I say? 'Hey, how would you like to upgrade to the meal deal for two?' Even the classic, 'Do you come here often?' can be neatly answered by, 'Of course, it's the fucking supermarket.'

I cannot feel sexually excited in the wash of artificial light amongst endless shelves of mass-produced, chemically-enhanced poisons in packaging that never rots. All I feel is the struggle between my desire for an easy life and the anxiety that our consumerist society is heading for collapse. The system is overloading. Like the folkloric German tale of *The Magic Porridge Pot*, the flow of foodstuffs just keeps coming and coming. I look at all the ham laid out in the refrigerated food aisle and realise that this is the same in every supermarket, service station, retail park and convenience store across the country. I can never get over the omnipresence of ham. How can so much of it exist simultaneously? Where are all the pigs for this ham? There should be pig farms spread across every inch of the country, just to keep this amount of ham flowing, or secret chambers beneath our cities, where pigs boil and perpetually whirring blades turn their corpses into wafer-thin slices. How can there be enough for everyone, everywhere, all the time? Not only ham but the chickens, the peas, the prawns, the cucumbers, the milk, the bread, the pasta sauces and biscuits in all their endless brand varieties. This cannot continue, I think, pushing my brimming trolley to the sound of a Boyzone ballad. We are doomed, and we deserve it. Quite frankly, in this kind of mood, the chance of me embarking on a flirty conversation with a stranger that results in sexual congress is virtually zero.

That's just me, of course. It appears that some people feel comfortable enough in supermarkets to talk to strangers and have sex with them afterwards. According to Asda's own survey, 'Pulse of the Nation', nearly half of their customers claim they've met potential partners in supermarkets. However, this 'fact' was used to advertise their own speed dating events, which took place across eighty of their stores in 2012. Perhaps a little more objective was a study by shopper marketing app Shopitize, which found that six per cent of those surveyed had dated someone they met in a supermarket. Saturday is apparently the best day for women to seek out men, while Tuesday night is ideal for men to meet women, with Morrisons topping the chart for best women-to-men ratio. Shopitize's survey responders admitted that the food in the other person's basket influenced their decision to date. In 2016, Tesco ran an experiment at their Hemel Hempstead Extra store in which subjects carried out their ideal purchases for a Friday night in, after which food behaviour psychologist Rachel Morris analysed their shopping, then used this information to help them find a romantic match. 'Our shopping baskets can say a lot about us,' she stated in the press release. 'We've all heard about love in the aisles and this is the next step.'

There's love to be found in the aisles of hardware superstores too, among the drills, plungers and dado rails. 'B&Q has almost been like a private members' club for lesbians,' wrote Julie Bindel in *The Guardian* in 2015[8], after news broke that sixty stores were going to close. 'Many a Sapphic romance has developed in B&Q. Nothing signifies more clearly that the woman in a checked shirt looking at spirit levels on a Sunday morning neither has a man at home, nor indeed wants one.' I have a lesbian friend who nodded fervently when I asked her if this was true. 'Oh yes, yes that's a thing,' she said, adding with a grin, 'B&Q stands for Bisexual and Queer.'

Of course, that's the world of the store interior. Out in the car park, things get weirder. In 2014, the *Bedfordshire News* revealed that the Sainsbury's car park in Dunstable was a top country hotspot for watching strangers have sex in cars, otherwise known as dogging. A couple of years later, *The Mirror* shared twenty-one popular dogging locations, including the Tower Retail Park in Crayford,

8   J. Bindel, 'The decline of B&Q is a hammer blow for lesbians', *The Guardian* online, 31 March 2015

south London, the Nugent Retail Park in Orpington, and the rear of the car park at Iceland in Petts Wood, Kent, where the action would kick off at 1 a.m. on weekdays or 2 a.m. at the weekend. A participant told the newspaper that some of the drivers from a nearby taxi firm would occasionally join in.

One Friday night, Kieran Davis, owner of a boxing club in Oxford, is parked outside Mothercare when he notices a nearby Vauxhall Corsa rocking. He realises that there is a couple having sex inside, so he does what any reasonable, sane person would do. He takes out his phone and streams the shagging on Facebook, a feed that is viewed 250,000 times. Some question the legality of filming people without consent. He later tells the *Oxford Mail*: 'I don't regret filming it and putting it on Facebook and I'm hoping it will be a deterrent – they were in the wrong place at the wrong time being exhibitionists and they should have kept it private.' After a while with his camera aimed at them, Davis informs the couple that they are on Facebook Live. Pulling up their underwear, they stumble out of the vehicle and call him a pervert. They have a point. Who are the perverts? People having public sex, or the man filming strangers having sex? Similarly, there are images splashed across Facebook and Twitter in 2015 of a couple allegedly having sex in the car park of the Bluewater Shopping Centre. Again, who is morally superior? The shagging couple, or the retweeters, sharers and newspapers who repeat the story with salacious glee? Or let's go one step further. Who is weirder? Me writing about people who film people banging in car parks? Or the people filming people banging in car parks?

Then there is the darker side of car park lust. Not long after we met, my wife told me about a friend of hers from Goldsmiths University who was accosted by a man in broad daylight outside a busy Sainsbury's in New Cross, south London. He was led at knifepoint to the rear of the store where he was raped. It's shocking, or used to be. I'm not so sure any more. A car park is an ideal place for a predator to scout for prey, in full view yet anonymous, part of the hustle and bustle. To look awkward in a car park is to look like pretty much everyone else. People of all shapes, sizes, ethnicities, classes, psychological states and demeanours use supermarkets. There is no official type against which you might stand out. Your size, your dress sense, your skin colour, your gender, your glazed eyes, your irritable expression, your weird, shuffling gait. None of these things mark you out as someone to watch for. Everyone blends in, making the place ripe for opportunists.

In 2013, a man exposes his genitals to two teenagers outside Norwich Morrisons. Another is arrested for indecent exposure in a Newport Morrisons. In Derbyshire, a woman loading her shopping into her boot senses something moving behind her and turns to see a stocky teenager holding up her skirt and taking a photo with his phone. In Plymouth, a twenty-one-year-old man is busted on camera having sex with a thirteen-year-old girl in the stairwell of the Toys R Us car park. In 2013, a man of thirty-seven grooms an underage girl on Facebook, luring her to the supermarket in Pontypool where he works, then having sex with her in the car park. Outside the Birchwood Shopping Centre ASDA, a forty-nine-year-old man is caught on CCTV masturbating in his vehicle as he watches shoppers enter the store, treating the car park as a live porno drive-through. In a Chester Tesco, an off-duty postman is caught doing the five-finger-shuffle. He later tells a court that he is 'sexually frustrated'. It's the obvious answer, I suppose. Less so for the man in a Swindon Homebase car park, found naked with a bag of cocaine under his foreskin, delirious with drugs and alcohol. I'll be honest. I feel more empathy for him than anyone who goes on an Asda speed dating evening. If it comes to the crunch, I'll probably end up being the Swindon Homebase guy.

NATURE CONSERVATION AREA

Tesco Stores Ltd: working to promote Biodiversity in Warwick

Chapter Twenty-Two
The Nature of Tesco

The traumatic collapse of my marriage is a Black Swan event. An outlier from nowhere. A total surprise that I do not expect, that I did not predict, and which strikes with terrible force, leaving nothing but a smoking crater. Coming as it does in the year of Brexit and Trump, I feel unshackled from the world I knew, flung into a wilderness without map or compass, there to face whatever strange new entities lurk in the undergrowth. In the spirit of the times, I decide to leave the familiar routes and use a spare weekend to test my proposition that any retail car park can be of interest by visiting one entirely at random. A car park to which I have never been, in a town which I have never visited, with no research to influence my choice. Geographically, it feels appropriate to pick a location in the Midlands. Somewhere central. I'm on the M40, en route to visit a friend in Staffordshire, when I see an exit sign for Warwick, a market town in the heart of Shakespeare country. It seems as good a place as any to visit.

I drive down a long high street of independent shops in buildings with wooden beams and pitched roofs, until I am out the other side of the town centre, when a sign for *Tesco: Open 24 Hours* directs me to turn right. As I descend into the car park, I pass a canal running underneath the bridge.

There's a narrowboat with four women drinking booze on deck, while on the towpath a man in shorts and a pink polo shirt holds a mooring rope in one hand and a glass of wine in the other. A swan waddles blithely towards him. I park across the road from in the Tesco filling station, next door to an ARC car wash, loud with hissing.

A zebra crossing with a smashed Belisha beacon offers me safe passage to a bus stop for the supermarket, with steps behind it leading down to the main car park. But I am intrigued by an electricity pylon further down the road. It overlooks a concrete mini-roundabout upon which stands a metal sign: ANPR (*automatic number plate recognition*) OPERATION IN PROGRESS. The pylon is the first leading from an electricity substation, a forest of vertical Dalek plungers behind steel slat fencing. In a strip of woodland protecting the substation from the road, they've planted saplings, which are all tilted in the same direction, at the same angle, as if they've been vandalised by someone with OCD. A sign proclaims that this is a Tesco *nature conservation area*, with the slogan, *Tesco Stores Ltd: working to promote biodiversity in Warwick*. Beneath the sign is a discarded plastic Tesco carrier bag, the text of which declares *the sale of every bag like me will help good causes*, except, it seems, the battle against plastic pollution. I cannot see what they mean by 'conservation area'. It seems a stretch to use this term to describe a copse between a filling station and a substation.

Things become clearer after I enter the car park and pass the Click & Collect zone to the far corner, where another pylon looms over a mildewed trolley bay. There is a pedestrian exit with *Goodbye: thank you for shopping with us* written on a sign obscured by thistles. Lilac bushes form a leafy corridor that leads me to a chocolate-brown river flowing through woodland towards a low railway bridge.

Car Park Life

Overhead power lines are reflected in the water as it eddies around discarded tyres, dead trees and a thick pipe looping out of the muddy bank. A sign shows me that I am in Emscote Nature Conservation Area on the site of a former power station on the River Avon. The huge quantities of sand used for the power station created a dune landscape that sprouted spiky marram grass after the power station closed and its servicing railway lines were abandoned. This became the habitat of hundreds of plant and invertebrate species. Tesco have instigated what the sign calls 'positive management' to maintain the diversity of the habitats while keeping the reserve navigable for visitors. The information sign is branded with the Tesco logo (*Every Little Helps*), and shows the animals I might find here, including solitary wasps, dragonflies, kingfishers, bats and otters.

I'm startled to find myself in this landscape so suddenly after leaving the car park. Even more so beside a Tesco sign that suggests this is an extension of the supermarket exterior. Supermarkets are usually desperate to build on brownfield sites, but in this case Tesco is a poacher-turned-gatekeeper. It's unlike anything I've seen so far in my explorations and goes to show what can be found when you depart from the well-worn holloways of daily life; or perhaps this is what happens when your spouse leaves you. A strange new world of possibilities opens up. Either way, it's exciting. This was a car park picked at random and I have ended up in a branded edgeland wilderness that I could not have predicted and certainly didn't expect. At any moment a black swan will drift into view.

I probe further beneath the bridge, then down a path alongside a metal fence entwined with bindweed. A roaring train sparks a cacophony of crow caws as a butterfly dances over a chocolate bar wrapper near a dog turd wrapped in plastic. This fusion of the synthetic and natural, the machine and the organic, is typical of the 'bastard landscape' I know from my days walking by the River Lea in the Hackney and Walthamstow Marshes. I've been lured into the same semi-industrial fairyland that inspired me to start writing about landscapes, which led me to explore retail car parks, and ultimately to this book. Things have come full circle. I'm back where it all began, albeit in a different place, geographically speaking. But for me, the joy of landscape is more than the location itself, it is about a state of mind in which you see the magic, weirdness and terror that runs through every particle, every atom, of the universe. It isn't only there in the spooky forest and the abandoned fairground, the canal and the summer meadow. It's in the mundane, everyday places where people work, play and live, even those monopolised by corporations with an interest only in profiting from you. It's in the suburban cul-de-sac. The tacky amusement arcade. The industrial estate. The alleyway behind your house. The car park of your nearest superstore. That's how a Tesco in Warwick can be as interesting as a London marshland or a Nepalese mountain.

On my return, an algae-smeared sign welcomes me back to Tesco. The superstore looms, stark and angular, electricity pylons reflected in its windows, as crows flap out across the sky. While Tesco's influence has spread into the wilderness, the process has worked in the opposite direction. The building is in a ragged state. The car-park-facing side contains the usual giant photos of foodstuffs, but they're in various states of decay. There are strips torn in the image of roast beef, as if it has been clawed at by a hungry bear. There's a rip in the new potatoes. The olives are barely visible at all, more whiteness than green. Even plastic and glass must succumb to the ravages of time, light and atmosphere. There is no denying nature. It is not separate to supermarkets, motorways, houses and car parks. It doesn't disappear when we tarmac it over. There is a creeping garden beneath us, seeking an opportunity to flourish in the cracks of things we build. It hides in darkness, waiting for light. We can hack it back, douse it with poison, cement over it, but it never relents. There is no respite, not even in the car park, not even on the side of this Tesco in Warwick.

As I take photos of the ruined food images, a taxi driver leans out of the window and asks me what I am doing.

'Taking photos,' I say, for want of a more interesting reply.

'You're going to replace them?' He means the images.

'No,' I said, 'I just find them interesting.'

He stares at me for a while, trying to work out if I am joking. I wonder if I am too. Then, after a few more seconds, I nod politely, slip my phone into my back pocket, and return to the car.

———————

The Warwick Tesco nature reserve is symptomatic of a trade-off between retail space and the natural environment. It's a means of the supermarket fulfilling a local social responsibility, which gives it developmental rights while extending its psychological influence beyond its boundaries. It's similar to the way the Penrith Sainsbury's Common Square Gardens has been positioned as a gateway to the old town, providing parking, taking a financial burden for constructing buildings and walkways but, in doing so, branding Penrith with Sainsbury-ness.

However, there's a positive side to the Tesco nature reserve. If we accept the necessity of the retail premises, and therefore the necessity of the car park, this is one way it could fulfil an environmentally positive function, instead of contributing to the unfolding eco-catastrophe. It could lessen the impact of what we are doing to the planet instead of creating its own disruptions. For instance, there is even such a thing as *car park weather*. In 2011, a supermarket worker named Alastair Brown filmed a twister in an IKEA car park at the Braehead shopping complex in Renfrewshire, Scotland. It span through the car park, whirling up dust and debris, dodging between vehicles. The STV weather presenter, Sean Batty, explained that it was 'a local wind effect, similar to a dust devil, that starts on the ground and travels upwards.' The heated tarmac on a warm day caused the air to lift in an anticlockwise rotation, creating suction beneath it. On a warming planet, where urban areas are increasingly dominated by car parks, roads, roofs and runways, this could become a regular phenomenon unless we decide to change the design and materials we use. Options include seeding car parks, shading them with trees and using more reflective surfaces.

We could also let life back in. A year after the twister, a foot-long lizard was spotted in a Bedfordshire Tesco car park. It had escaped from a nearby house and sought refuge up a tree. A few members of staff managed to lure the beast into a box and call a local pet store to rescue it. A spokeswoman for Tesco told the media: 'We always say that "Everyone is Welcome" at Tesco, but we draw a line at reptiles!' I am not sure this is the right thing to say. Surely there is room for reptiles in the era of global warming, sunning themselves in the heat on the fringes of car parks, feasting on insects in wild flower verges. If we don't allow this, it will only quicken the events that lead to a similar situation anyway, except it will be a human-free Galapagos of creatures crawling over our remnants, making homes in superstore ruins, screaming from the rooftops of derelict malls, swinging from our pylons.

Birds are already moving into the superstore space. In Cheadle, a Sainsbury's is the annual nesting ground for Canada geese, who lay their eggs near the petrol station forecourt. The management puts a cordon around the area to stop cars parking, so that they can nest undisturbed. A 2008 article on the BirdGuides website enthused about the rise in waxwing sightings in supermarket car parks. It said: 'Even if you feel out-of-town superstores are responsible for the decline of Britain's high streets and the loss of scrubby local patches rich in warblers and finches, there's no doubt that retail car parks are the place to look for these denizens of the northern forests.' The winter of 2005–06 was a bumper year, with twenty per cent of reporting sightings in supermarket car parks, the largest number of which were in Morrisons[9]. The suggestion was that Sir Ken Morrison, a keen birdwatcher, was so keen on his three billion pound takeover of Safeway because it would help him top the waxwing charts.

Fascinated by this phenomenon, I scour the web for more testimony. On one forum, a birdwatcher claims to have spotted the following in his local car park during the winter: 'robin, blackbird, dunnock, wren, magpies, woodpigeon, pied wagtail, blue tit, great tit, coal tit, long tailed tit, greenfinch, chaffinch, carrion crow, lesser black backed gulls and fieldfare and redwing'. A worker in a Glasgow Morrisons claims he once spotted over a hundred waxwings in the car park. Another says that their retail complex is full of shrubs which are home to sparrows and blackbirds. Starlings are increasingly adapting their behaviour to suit car parks, realising that humans mean

9   *Bird Guides*, www.birdguides.com/articles/mums-gone-to-finland, 31 December 2008

food. A forum user writes that they've seen starlings in the car parks of service stations on the M1 making a direct line for newly arrived cars, so that they can feast on a front bumper smorgasbord of dead insects.

I confront my own ornithological spectacular at Tottenham Hale Retail Park one morning after I step out from the Premier Inn, where I've spent the night after a gig. I fancy a walk by the River Lea but I need a coffee first. The retail park's sail-shaped sign beckons me into its plaza of brand names. I pass a Next window containing Aryan child mannequins with Midwich Cuckoo stares, then an empty store with the word CAPITAL and a silhouette of St Paul's Cathedral, crossed out by masking tape, plastered on the window. In the Costa, I knock back a double espresso. Upon exiting, I notice a black and white bird bobbing along the walkway. Then another perched on the bin. Suddenly, there are almost a dozen pied wagtails hopping at the feet of oblivious shoppers. I am so accustomed to pigeons and gulls in car parks that these birds seem exotic, a taste of a lost paradise. Further on there's a flock of starlings, exhibiting no fear as they approach cars or weave between pedestrians. On a bench, a couple of crows look on approvingly. In the anxiety of a hangover, this gathering feels like a prelude to Hitchcockian horror. At my feet I spot a square concrete sewer hatch in the paving slabs, with a hole in its centre and the text EARTH ROD. It suggests a connection between land and sky, between this concrete plateau and the wild, primordial ooze beneath it. A starling flaps out across the parked cars and I wonder what it all means.

A year later, I read a tweet by the author Sarah Perry, marvelling at a flock of pied wagtails at the Norwich Morrisons, and ask her if it is worth a visit, thinking about this chapter of the book, and how a majestic vision of wildlife in the contemporary retail space will hammer home my point. 'Yes!' she replies. So I take up an invitation to read at the Norwich launch of an anthology in which one of my stories appears. It is the summer of 2018 – the big heatwave. In the weeks before the event, fire rages on Saddleworth Moor, exacerbated by the dry conditions. Later that month, wildfires ravage Greece, California, and even forests inside the Arctic Circle. A study in *Nature* declares that the melting of the Antarctic ice sheet has tripled in five years. Two other studies are published, one predicting that coral reefs will soon be overwhelmed by rising sea levels and another that the vulnerable ice shelves will accelerate the process. We are beyond the tipping point, say the scientists, and there is no possibility of return. Appropriately, the short story I read at the book launch depicts two women who live together on a crumbling cliff in East Sussex twenty years from now, watching storm tides battering Dungeness power station, waiting for the end of the world, a scenario that feels imminent this summer. The next morning, I walk down a hill from my hotel to the superstore, my eyes sore with a combination of hangover pain and sunshine, heat shimmering the road, wobbling the railway line, solid structures seemingly melting all around me.

The Morrisons forms part of a large retail park beside the football stadium. I hope to confront inspirational numbers of birds chattering in the trees, but all I see are the ubiquitous green rat traps lining the perimeter wall, desire lines through the shrubs, the mud turned to dust, a billboard for a dry cleaning service depicting a besuited couple with no heads, and a poster for a local business, INANNA'S MAGICAL GIFTS, offering a selection of fairies, mermaids, dragons, crystals, gemstones and tarot readings. A woman in black smokes a cigarette on a bench, tapping on her phone as a staff member rearranges some plastic Union flags over a display of pot plants. I don't know why I've assumed I'll discover a Garden of Eden in Norwich, but that's how my stupid brain works. I listen hard for chirping and twittering but the ambience is a blend of car engines, trolley wheels and the bleep of automatic doors. A promising pathway at the back of the store is bordered by a slope of wood chippings and silver birch trees, but no birds. Perhaps it is the wrong time of day, the wrong time of year. I trudge across the tarmac, passing some bird-less pine trees towards the valeting station, with its forest of jet wash poles. Then I see it where I least expect, perched on the Perspex covering of the trolley bay: a pied wagtail. Only one. A solitary bird. But I feel an extraordinary surge of relief. It is only one pied wagtail, but it's *something*. A small mercy, dancing on a plastic dome.

In November 2016, a shopper films a giant rat with a doughnut in its mouth racing across the car park of a Krispy Kreme in an Oldham retail park, before it is attacked by a herring gull. It makes the tabloid news. The sight is nothing new for my friend, Martin Fuller, a film-maker from London who has taken to watching rats at Lidl in Mile End. They're in constant movement in a wedge of space between the car park wall and the canal where shoppers toss their rubbish, waiting for closing time to come and clean up what's left. Above them, a flock of scraggy pigeons keeps a constant vigil on a guano-coated railing beneath the store sign. When the sixth Great Extinction hits its destructive apex, perhaps only a few decades from now, this might be the only filmable nature left for an Attenborough-style documentary to cover. *Life on Car Park Earth*. Ten episodes, one for each of the remaining species.

We are reaching the end of the show. The car park is the final stage. Then, I'm afraid, it's curtains.

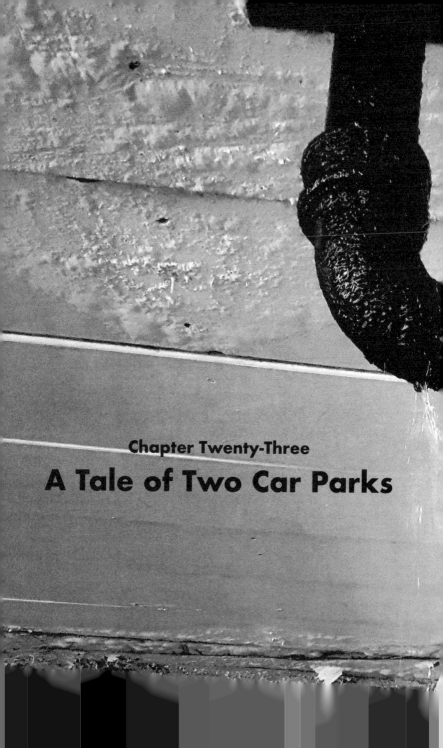

Chapter Twenty-Three

A Tale of Two Car Parks

You write one story about having sex with an electricity pylon, then suddenly you're 'the pylon guy'. That's what happened to me when my short story 'A Dream Life of Hackney Marshes' was published. It was about a real pylon for which I genuinely felt affection, but I can categorically say, Bill Clinton-style, that I did not have sexual relations with that pylon. No fluids were exchanged. I might have licked it once, briefly – nothing more than the tip of my tongue – primarily for the sense of danger, rather than arousal, and I regretted it immediately afterwards. The story was less about the fetishisation of an object and more about how my fascination for the ugly landscape of the Anthropocene feels illicit, dirty, even thrilling. A band called Jetsam based a concept album on my story, including 'Angel', a love song to the pylon with me on vocals[10], which we recorded at the University of Huddersfield.

The result of exposing my pylon love in public was that I became a go-to guy whenever someone on social media found a pylon story, a pylon gif or a piece of pylon art. Each time I shared or liked a pylon photo that I had been sent, I became more *pylonic* in the eyes of others, and more likely to receive more pylons, thus more likely to pass them on. These fetishes

10   *A Dreamlife Of Hackney Marshes* was released by Clay Pipe Music in 2013.

gain their own momentum, carrying you on an ascending wave. But I wasn't arrogant enough to think I was 'the pylon guy' when there were many more obsessive people running pylon-related Twitter feeds, blogs, Facebook communities, forums and God knows what else. For me, pylons represented a way of thinking about, and looking at, landscape.

This is how it is with chain store car parks. I am not sure if my experiences and thoughts are shared by others, or if they're the effect of a troubled mind. What will happen when I broadcast these ideas? Will I tap into a hidden vein of enthusiasm, finding legions of fellow car park travellers, or will I be met with incredulity? Boredom? Hostility? Whatever my fears, I decide to declare my interest publicly before I write a whole book on the subject. So when I see a call for submissions for the '4th World Congress of Psychogeography' in Huddersfield, the place we recorded our pylon music, it feels like the stars have aligned. I offer to lead a group of attendees through the superstore car parks of Huddersfield and the organisers accept my proposal. Six months later, I am on the train north.

The 4th World Congress of Psychogeography consists of two days of lectures, performance and exploratory walks. A trailer for my event in the *Huddersfield Examiner* begins: 'It may sound like the world's most boring walk but a tour of Huddersfield supermarket car parks this Sunday promises to be anything but dull.' As I have not yet visited the car parks I'm about to tour, I have no idea about that, but confidence is key. I cannot show that I'm riddled with doubt, which is why I turn up wearing a T-shirt that reads:

**MY PSYCHOGEOGRAPHY IS
BETTER THAN
YOUR PSYCHOGEOGRAPHY**

Car Park Life

I spend the first day at the back of a room in the bowels of the university, feeling self-conscious about the T-shirt, trying to suss out how amenable the crowd might be to my car park odyssey. There are people here whose work I have read, including Dr Morag Rose, Dr Tina Richardson, Roy Bayfield and Sonia Overall. There's Phil Smith too, the man behind 'mythogeography', a methodology that subverts, reimagines or corrupts the images encountered on a walk to create new myths, encouraging people to seek out the magic in the ordinary, and empowering them to tell their own stories. Smith seeks out meanings in the juxtapositions of signs and symbols, on packaging, road markings, corporate logos and the Rorschach splatters of paint, piss and oil. He has a thing for car parks too. Back in 2004, he and Matthew Watkins conducted an experimental performance called *The Gap*, in which they applied the geometric principles of the Victorian mathematician William Kingdon Clifford to the car parks of Exeter. So I listen closely as he takes the stage and says:

> There's a famous suggestion that, in our discourses and entertainments, we find it easier to imagine the end of the world than the end of capitalism. But that's not true. In fact, we find it wholly possible to imagine an end both to capital and to human life – there are long lists of apocalyptic and post-apocalyptic fictions in which both cease to 'be' – what we find difficult is acting as if anything of any worth would follow.

Smith says that in this period of human history where progress is stumbling, and the end of the world as we know it seems imminent, we have an opportunity to take a fresh look around us and 'defend certain freedoms, spaces, remaining autonomies'. We can do this, he suggests, by going on a pilgrimage. Not an aimless wander, but a deliberate search for 'channels and corridors in public space, safe passage hidden in plain sight'. These places aren't always where you expect, says Smith. 'You only find a hidden sanctuary by testing for it.'

Is that what I've been doing? Probing for hidden sanctuaries in the urban consumer landscape? Am I on a pilgrimage through retail car parks? If so, how do I know when I achieve my destination? How do I know when to stop?

'There is no destination,' explains Smith in his talk, by way of an answer. 'There is no shrine, the only holy thing is the unfolding road.'

I have been seeking the magical possibilities of bland corporate space in the hope that there is a potential channel of escape from neo-liberal hegemony, even if that escape is purely psychological and subjective, a new way of seeing the urban landscape foisted upon us, and embracing it in a way that offers a possibility of a future, no matter how bleak the situation, no matter how inevitably we must reap the coming whirlwind of fascism, global warming and ecological collapse. So I get what Phil Smith is saying. The point is not that I discover a divine secret about retail car parks, nor locate some holy grail, but that I undergo a spiritual personal transformation. That is the only measure of success. More importantly, that we all attempt to undergo this process, in our own landscapes, in our own ways and in our own time, no matter whether we choose industrial estates, the Lake District, our local bus network, the Mayan ruins of Mexico or the daily walk to work. The focus of our attention makes no difference. Meadows or motorways, grass or concrete, strawberries or Styrofoam, orchids or pyracantha, rubber plants or rubber johnnies. They are all things of the universe, made of matter, energy and empty space, with all the elements of the universe contained within them, and all the mystery too. It isn't the objects that must change, but our view of them, and our view of ourselves in relation to them. We are not separate. We are not superior. We are not exempt. These things are us and we are these things. When enough human beings realise this truth, we may have the potential for change, if not to avert eco-disaster, then to live with it as well as we can, enlightened and at peace with the cosmos.

———————

After the talks, I check into my Premier Inn, situated on the canal between the university and a Sainsbury's, which I've pegged as the first destination on my tour. The receptionist is incredibly friendly and asks me why I'm in Huddersfield. I explain that I'm here to lead strangers on a tour of car parks to which I've never been. He shows no surprise. 'Oh, well this is an interesting one we're in right now,' he says, 'this hotel and the Sainsbury's car park are in Aspley Wharf or, as it used to be known, the armpit of Huddersfield, on account of all the coal being offloaded here by the barges.'

See? Everyone has a car park story.

The next day, torrential rain. I wear a waterproof, which means nobody sees the MY PSYCHOGEOGRAPHY IS BETTER THAN YOUR PSYCHOGEOGRAPHY T-shirt. At the university, a group of around twenty listen patiently as I roar through an account of my Morrisons epiphany, the night that began it all. After, we file in a murmuring procession along the canal towpath and up the road to Sainsbury's. As the rain finally eases we congregate on grass at the main entrance beside a billboard with aspirational images of the sort of people Sainsbury's want to attract to their stores, wearing clothes from Sainsbury's own range. However, the sort of people this particular Sainsbury's wants to attract are not the usual Sainsbury's shoppers because this is a Sainsbury's that dreams it's a Waitrose. Well-dressed, mainly Caucasian, shoppers stroll politely between their cars and the pillared frontage. Phil Wood, one of the event organisers, and also a local, tells me that there is no Waitrose in or near Huddersfield, so the more well-to-do folk come to this regenerated history-scape, away from the town centre, where an eclectic array of garden plants welcomes arrivals. The superstore is constructed in sandstone sympathetic to the Victorian mill landscape along the route of the canal, in the municipal style exemplified by the Sainsbury's in Penrith, with the same eagerness to integrate with the local industrial heritage as the Asda in Leith's dockland. As the Civic Society chairman Chris Marsden said in 2016: 'Sandstone is as fundamental to the character of Huddersfield as limestone is to the Cotswolds, granite is to Aberdeen and flint is to East Anglia[11].'

Spoiling this effect somewhat is a shipping container behind the billboard with a limp flag advertising a car washing service. The container is closed. There are bulges in the steel, as if someone, or something, has been trying to kick its way out. I put my ear against it to listen for the muffled cries of gagged captives. There's a group of people with me this time, of course. Watching me. Expecting me to have some idea of what's going on. So I lead them along

11 *Huddersfield Examiner*, 20 Jan 2016

the slope by the railings like a pound shop Jesus heading for the mount. In this case, the mount is a trolley bay. Behind the Perspex there's a stack of trolleys, one of which contains a dozen empty cider bottles. I don't know what it means. I ask if anyone knows what it means. Nobody knows what it means. I am not the car park Christ they were hoping for. Part of me wishes that the cider bottles were full of piss. Then that would be something.

At the farthest corner I stop the group again beside a raised bed, empty of plants but containing a discarded Actimel bottle, beer can, coat hanger and sodden polo shirt. There's a story here, I announce, hoping someone will tell me what it is. And they do, with gusto. It looks like someone stole a garment from Sainsbury's and left behind their old clobber, quickly downing a can of lager for courage, then Actimel out of guilt. Beside the wall there's a bin for road salt. Someone opens it. The salt is stained yellow with – yes, at last – piss, and lots of it. It reeks. This is the underbelly of the car park that the Waitrose-wannabe Sainsbury's doesn't want us to see. The group are into it now, I can tell. It's the cracks in the facade that make car parks interesting. The stories you put together yourself. Anyone can do it.

The pissy salt and stolen goods are not the only sign of trouble. A wooden barrier between the car park and the access road has been smashed. A desire path has formed where people have walked through the gap, down the verge and across the access road. Did this barrier get broken first by a badly parked car, and then zombie pedestrians poured through it unthinkingly? Or did someone deliberately smash the barrier at this point? For what reason? On the other side of the access road is a tiny wedge of woodland, which may be the desired destination for whoever uses the unofficial exit path, but with twenty people behind me, and constant cars swooshing round the bend on this Saturday afternoon, I don't wish to risk crossing, so instead we proceed to the edge of the car park overlooking the canal towpath.

The view from here across to the superstore is remarkable. The building appears fused with the old mill building behind it, the redundant chimney seemingly rising from Sainsbury's roof, a wispy grey cloud above like the memory of the smoke it once emitted, with gasometers and pylons in the distance telling the story of the past century. The wall of the canalside is also the wall of the car park, with stone steps leading from the cars down to the narrowboats, where a dog barks by a pile of logs. At the side of the superstore building, where a walkway leads to the staff car park and delivery bays, Victorian style gas lamps protrude from the wall, imbuing it with a Dickensian quality, like a scene from *Hard Times*. On the surface, the supermarket looks more 'heritage' than what is on the other side of the canal – the real industrial architecture, characterised by a black warehouse, shipping containers, traffic cones and coiled wire fencing. The Sainsbury's is a cartoon version of 'authentic' juxtaposed with the real thing. As the film-maker Patrick Keiller once wrote:

> Capitalism both destroys and creates places, but the places it creates seem always, at least to begin with, less substantial, less rich, than the places it destroys – as in the case of, say, the mechanisation of agriculture and the ports, or the replacement of mining and other industries by landscape of distribution and retailing[12].

---

12 P. Keiller, 'Popular Science' in *Informal Architecture: Space and Contemporary Culture*, ed. A. Kiendl, Kiendl, Black Dog Publishing 2008 Black Dog Publishing 2008

Car Park Life

Huddersfield Sainsbury's is a reconstructed version of the previous landscape, implying a connection with the past that wasn't there. As my friend at the Premier Inn said, this was the armpit of Huddersfield, piled high with coal, thick with smoke, in a time before industrial edgelands became picturesque enough to be a selling point for supermarkets.

Since the Second World War, commerce has increasingly taken over our urban space. Superstores have appropriated civic halls, cinemas and pubs, or filled the gaps left by demolished factories, tower blocks and churches. When space ran out for new buildings and car parks, developers looked out of town at edgeland sites, brownfield land and ring roads, creating superstores that offered everything under one roof for the convenience of the motorist. This trend has slowed and development has returned to our towns in zones like this one in Huddersfield, with space for parking, existing structures to repurpose and a history that gives the store gravitas and credibility. The 'everything under one roof' principle has been brought back into our urban centres, with superstores offering prescription services, banking, laundry, currency exchange, recycling and charity collections. In some towns they have become the only remaining vestiges of the marketplace, the village green, the parish hall, the old high street, places where people gather, exchange stories, trade wares, fall in love, fight, gossip, screw and settle scores. This behaviour is not always visible, and rarely permitted, but life always finds a way. We can see it in this Sainsbury's frontage, which looks like a village high street, with a pharmacy, cash machine, passport photo booth, key cutting and dry cleaning. It would have startled a Victorian barge worker to see this on the dirty dockside of Huddersfield. However, he would have been far less surprised about the location of the Tesco, a different car park entirely.

It takes the group ten minutes to walk up the ring road to the northern edge of Huddersfield town centre, where the Tesco is situated across the road from the indoor market. Tesco began as a market stall and this building harks back to its ancestor business, with a covered area created by the two-storey car park upon which the store sits. In front of the entrance steps, a butcher bellows the latest offers from his wagon, while at the top of those same steps, a couple of drunken blokes blather on a bench.

The shoppers are more working class and ethnically diverse than in the Sainsbury's. Lots of brown and black faces. A mixture of accents. And unlike the polite veneer of Sainsbury's, there's tension up here, caused by limited parking space on the busiest shopping day of the week. The corners are tight with no room for mistakes. Traffic is backing up all around the rooftop. The more cars queuing, the less space there is for other cars to reverse out. A line of stationary vehicles rumbles impatiently. From open windows voices shout, 'Come on!' and 'Hurry up!' as parents nervously guide their children between cars. It feels perilous to be up here as a group of twenty but this is the supermarket car park at peak time in all its glory, teeming with life. As the rain starts up again I can sense the roof groaning with the weight of it all. The tarmac looks like it's nearing the end of its lifespan, warped and buckled, dimples filled with rainwater, the parent-and-child parking bays faded, a headless boy holding the hand of his faded ghost mum. The white panelling of the store is also in decay, blackened by pollution. There is no attempt to integrate the structure into the sandstone Victoriana of industrial Huddersfield. No phony heritage here. This is a supermarket that knows it's a supermarket.

I lead the group in single file off the roof and down a steep car ramp, walking against the flow of traffic. We duck into the low, angled wedge of space beneath the ramp at the entrance to the covered car park, where we crouch for a while like sheltering Neanderthals. Others have been here recently. A coat hanger dangles from a nail in the wall above a rat trap and an espresso cup. There's a crushed can. A muddy boot print. A cigarette butt. Life creeps into these dark, dry corners. Within the cavernous interior, this is a nook of relative safety from where you can see your attackers coming.

We push deeper into the covered car park. The strains in the structure which I could see on the roof are even more evident down here. Fist-sized chunks of concrete lie scattered, surrounded by halos of dust, rusted iron supports exposed, bleeding orange down the white paint. There's a constant trickling of water, as if we have entered a subterranean cave system. Stalactites hang from the ceiling, beaded with moisture. On a support pillar, the word 'rain' is daubed in electric blue lettering, a discarded umbrella lying below it. This is a synchronous juxtaposition. These two objects are in conversation, interrelating somehow, beyond the understanding of humans.

On the back wall there is more graffiti, where teenagers on bikes do wheelies and a body shifts irritably inside a sleeping bag. I don't consider leading the tour group past the homeless person. Too intrusive and voyeuristic. We are not only trespassing on Tesco property, using it for purposes other than shopping, but on these people's lives too, in the place they call home, albeit temporary and unofficial.

We move instead to a section of the car park near the lifts, where two lads smoke joints and snigger as our group shuffles past. There is more decay here. Fissures in the concrete, wires protruding. Water drips, trickles, seeps. A black wall is streaked with lines of ochre. On an overhang above the central parking bays, numbers have been hand-drawn in felt-tip pen. Builders leaving repair notes? Or code used by the subterranean car park dwellers? By now I am asking these questions only of myself, as the group has dispersed throughout the space, taking photos, as if in the catacombs of an ancient cathedral, lost in their own reveries. I'm pleased that they find it fascinating. This is a superstore car park unlike any I've yet explored and I feel the buzz of seeing something new in a familiar landscape. For me, the true discovery is rarely the place itself – a location on a map or a building – but in understanding empirically that there are worlds hidden in plain sight, which can become visible if we bother to lift our veils and see the Britain that is, not an idealised Britain that never was.

Despite my best intentions to make sense of car park life, I am just as myopic as anyone else. What I don't realise at the time is that I have led this group of people within thirty feet of a dead body. Not in the Tesco, where you might prejudicially expect this might happen, but in the genteel heritage Sainsbury's we explored earlier. A few weeks after my Huddersfield tour, a decomposing body is found in the wedge of woodland between the canal and the Sainsbury's, the one by the broken barrier that I didn't risk crossing with the group. It has been there for months and will have lain there as we all trooped by. Sad as it is, the revelation doesn't shock me as much as it should. Bodies often lie undiscovered in car parks. On the first of January 2014, the body of a priest, slumped over the steering wheel, was found outside a Morrisons in Houghton Regis. He had been there since 27 December. Nobody noticed, even at the busiest time of year. The Bishop of Northampton, Peter Doyle, said: 'I think it makes people feel guilty that we didn't look or that we didn't find him, but it was unavoidable and it's just one of those things.' That same year, the body of a fifty-year-old man was found outside a Tesco in Essex by a car park attendant who noticed a rotten smell. The man had been missing for a month. Police said that he was in the car park all that time. It happened again in January 2016, when a man was found dead in his vehicle at an Asda in Merseyside. A customer told the media, 'It was only noticed today. Obviously that may be because Saturday is a busier day, but I'm surprised no one noticed anything considering where the car is.'

The man found in Huddersfield was a Polish scaffolder, a gentle, kind man by all accounts. Nobody knows how he died, but whatever happened in those final hours, that patch of woodland must have felt dark and lonely, a wilderness only metres from civilisation, resonant with traffic noise and visitors coming and going from narrowboats, cars and the hotel. An island in an ocean of people too busy to listen, including me, striding around with a tour group, preoccupied with my viewpoint, feeding my own ego. If walking car parks is a pilgrimage, then I feel very far from enlightenment. Even when looking closely, I didn't see that deeper, darker layer of car park life and death. I missed the real story that was there, all the time.

Chapter Twenty-Four
The Waste Land

'I think we are in rats' alley
Where the dead men lost their bones.'
– T.S. Eliot, *The Waste Land*

For as long as the combustion engine and retail stores exist, there will be a need for space to park cars, and therefore car parks will endure. Unless I retire to a Highland bothy to grow vegetables and rear animals, it's a landscape I cannot avoid. But after years wandering them with my eyes peeled for secret lives and hidden histories, it's impossible to see them the way I used to. We never quite fell in love, but car parks and I have had a relationship, however dysfunctional. Even after the break-up necessitated by the completion of this book, car parks and I will continue to encounter each other in that awkward way you might bump into an ex-lover in the supermarket aisle, where you are assailed by memories of emotions, sensations and images, their soft gaze in candlelight, the touch of their skin, the tears and laughter, arguments, orgasmic moans, their breathing at night, the triumphs and disappointments. The memory of your connection never goes away, even when you are staring at the dried husk of what existed, little more than an outline of what used to be. That's me and car parks. Once an obsession has gripped you there's no escape. Even when you let go, there's a piece of you which has been irrevocably altered, like a Tesco built on a field in which you used to play. There won't be an end to *Car Park Life*, not for me. I understand that.

However, I get an odd feeling of finality this spring morning as I exit the A48 dual carriageway on the outskirts of Newport, South Wales, at the edge of the Severn Estuary. The first draft of this book is almost complete, but I figure that another walk won't do me any harm. I am not sure what I will find, but I have developed a skill for sniffing out car parks and I am rewarded with a sign for the Newport Retail Park, its silver serif car-showroom-style font luring me past a Tesco and into a cradle of blocks with stores like Marks & Spencer, H&M, Next, New Look and Outfit. It's a gleaming contemporary construction. Overhangs of glass and steel cast lattice shadows on marble slabs, silver bollards and sculpted metal benches. This retail park aspires to be a social hub as well as somewhere to shop. Outside Dorothy Perkins and Burton, concrete chairs are arranged at angles for the encouragement of conversation. Nobody sits on them. They're a monument to a society that has never existed out here on the ring road. In the TUI travel agency window, I can see the reflection of the car park in a photo of a tropical island scene, palm trees overlooking a golden beach, ghostly vehicles lined up in the surf.

For all its aspirations, there are cracks in the retail park's facade: a smashed reflector on a bollard, a dent in a metal post, an unoccupied store. There is nothing as embarrassing for the retail park as an empty shop. To compensate, they've covered the glass in the outlines of metropolitan shoppers in chinos and skirts. A sign above the door reads OUTLET, a generic placeholder name. I can make out the outline of the name of the store that was originally here – GAP – appropriately now an actual gap. This is the reality the Newport Retail Park is doing its best to make customers forget. They'd rather you focussed on the Marks & Spencer at the end of the block. But once I step around the side of Marks & Spencer, it looks monstrous suddenly – corrugated grey panels, stacks of containers and a caged generator with a *Danger of Death* sign. Once outside that gleaming square of fashion stores, a very different area of retail park opens out, consisting of warehouse-style retail buildings along shabby access roads. All the pretence has been stripped away. A Hyundai dealership's wall is a collage of ventilation fans and CCTV cameras. There's a backdrop of electricity pylons behind the roof of Home Bargains and a store called 4xercise 4 Less, all of which have their own car parks.

To access these stores, cars are flung out from a mini-roundabout formed of a circular pavement around a disc of lawn, surrounded by concentric rings of burned rubber left by late-night joyriders and cruisers. One direction leads to a Frankie & Bennys, but I take the road between the back of Marks & Spencer and the front of Home Bargains, where a van sells sandwiches to truck drivers and staff, proclaiming itself *The First Hot Baguette Trailer in Wales, supported by IBF World Champion Lee Selby*. I don't know much about Lee Selby, but if George Foreman can sell grills, I'm sure a Welsh boxer can get his weight behind steak sandwiches.

Beyond the van are the twin car parks of Peugeot and Citroen, then a fenced-off wasteland of nettles and briars, piled with mounds of earth, beyond which I can see a Matalan, hunkered like an abandoned farmhouse refuge in a savaged countryside. The road is only for visitors to that store, or delivery trucks entering the rear of Marks & Spencer and Asda, with weed-strewn pavement leading to a dead end. I feel conspicuous walking alone here, taking photos as if planning a heist.

At the Matalan car park, a sign warns that its gates will close at night, and I can see why. The tarmac is ringed with tyre marks. A dented lamp post leans from a crumbled concrete plinth, and shattered glass sparkles in the sun. This is a boy-racer track, I can see that immediately. There's a car wheel on its side near bushes littered with KFC and McDonald's packaging, the tossed detritus of onlookers as cars screech and billow smoke. A sweep of cigarette butts and joint roaches lies against the kerb among Rentokil death chambers. A pair of discarded trousers, torn at the knee, is being bleached gradually by the sun. The wrappers, butts, plastic bottles and cans intensify at a far corner of the car park fence where steel slats have been bent akimbo, as if by a circus strong man, offering passage into a dense area of trees. As I approach, there's a crash and crack, splintering wood, as something moves suddenly at speed through the undergrowth. My heart leaps. I look around in panic. Matalan is open but there is nobody in the car park, nobody who will notice if I disappear into this gap and never return. This fear is stupid. But I really feel it, I cannot deny. It takes almost a minute for me to gather myself and duck into the darkness.

The atmosphere is claustrophobic, steamy with odours of fungus, rotten wood and mouldering fabrics. Bulging plastic bags hang in tangled branches above piles of socks and shirts, torn bin liners and fragments of plastic tubing. I listen out for more movement but hear nothing except the ambient hiss of distant cars punctuated by crow caws. This is a hiding place, party zone or ritualistic site. There's a suspicious mound of soil, as if something has been hurriedly buried, and a circle of ash from a fire. I'm not sure why I feel such unease, only a few strides away from Matalan, but it's the proximity of this place to the retail park that disturbs me. A little further in, a water channel crusted with green algae. On the opposite bank is another fence, beyond which pylons roam. There is nowhere to run from here. Perhaps it was only a fox that I heard crashing through the foliage, or a form of miniature human, specially adapted to life in the wastelands of Matalan, lurking on the fringes of society like a dystopian Womble, feasting on what we throw away.

It may be that I am infected with the *genius loci* of this edgeland, or overwhelmed by empathy for those who choose to dwell here, but at this very moment I unzip my jeans and unleash an arc of piss into the undergrowth, as so many have done before. With valedictory steam rising in the cavity behind me, I return, blinking, to the car park, and follow the remainder of the road to the dead end, where a sign declaring *CCTV in Operation: No Fly-Tipping* is surrounded by an insulting amount of rubbish: flaps of carpet, plastic forks, Lucozade bottles, mounds of black plastic bags. Smashed TVs. Stained duvet draped on the kerb. Cardboard box on a tree branch. It's as if a dustbin lorry has exploded.

Beyond a battered gate, a footpath runs behind the Matalan store through an avenue of brambles. I don't particularly want to enter, but I can't turn away from a mystery. Inside the thicket, the air is dank and buzzing with so many flies that I half expect to see a human leg protruding from the undergrowth. Eventually the path widens, then bends left at a fence beneath the power lines, terminating at a padlocked steel gate with a concrete boulder in front of it. Journey's end, it seems. I look closer at the concrete boulder. An R has been spray painted on it, with a yellow arrow pointing to the right. This cannot be coincidence. Richard III was discovered beneath an R painted on a Leicester car park. I kick around the nettles at the foot of the fence where the arrow directs me. There's never a dead English king when you want one, is there? Perhaps it's not the verge that the R points to, but the pylons behind the fence. After all, I am a 'pylon guy' and my surname begins with R. Am I being told that I am on the right track in the scrubland behind Matalan? Or is it a warning that I am hopelessly off-track and far from where I should be? Or perhaps it means absolutely nothing. Why does anything have to mean anything? And why would a cosmic message be aimed at me anyway? I don't know. I just don't know. All I know is that it's here and I am looking at it.

> So much depends
> upon
>
> a block of grey
> concrete
>
> sprayed with
> paint
>
> behind the red
> supermarket.

That's the trouble with endings in non-fiction books like this one. You want revelations and conclusions, resolutions and epiphanies, but all you're going to get are more questions.

———————

When I return to my car from the Matalan wasteland, I'm surprised by the polished stone beneath my feet, the vertical garden on the wall of Nando's and the bright red umbrellas shading the al fresco tables of Pizza Express. It's all so shiny and new. Even my dented Peugeot hatchback feels luxurious as I climb into its interior. As the radio burbles into action I hear my first human voices in what seems an age. I have only been gone for an hour but it feels like I've travelled into the heart of darkness.

I drive down to the roundabout, from where I've just come, which now looks completely innocuous, like any retail park, and I turn right onto the road past Frankie & Bennys. To my dismay, there's an even larger secondary retail complex with McDonald's, Pizza Hut, Cineworld, Harvester and Indian buffet, among others, all with car parks, roundabouts and access roads. I should park and take a walk. But I'm tired. I feel sick. I can't do this any more. I think about the arrow on the concrete block, pointing to the pylons, and about the R in the car park in Leicester. Perhaps I should take heed of the sign and let pylons lead me away from this place.

With a sense of relief, I leave the retail park via Meadows Road, which follows the pylons south over the wetlands towards the estuary shore. As I pass Newport Motorpoint: The Car Supermarket and the Leeway Industrial Estate, I see thick smoke billowing into the blue sky. I pull up sharply at the entry to a cul-de-sac of trade businesses, Action Petz, BP Rolls and Jumbocruiser Ltd, surrounded by white vans. The field opposite is on fire. The land has been hacked into clods of soil, black earth bristling with dead stalk stubble. Pyres of vegetation blaze flame, smoke blotting out two motionless wind turbines, filthy cirrus wisps trailing over the pylon tops towards the Bristol Channel. The world is burning. We must confront this truth. I get out of the car, pulling my T-shirt over my mouth to filter the dirty air, and I watch for a while.

I'm in my mid-forties and, bad as everything is in the world right now, with forest fires inside the Arctic Circle, mass extinctions, and traces of plastic sluicing through our bodies, it's unlikely that civilisation will end before I die. The economic decline of the UK might contract the number of car parks and change the brand names. Perhaps Tesco, Sainsbury's, Asda and Morrisons will be replaced by the likes of Lidl and Aldi, which in turn will be replaced by some Chinese, American or Russian conglomerate, before our retail buildings become derelict husks sheltering ramshackle black markets where people exchange whatever they can salvage from the wreckage of western society – tins of beans and spam, blankets, batteries and torches. But while there is air in my lungs, there will be places to exchange some form of money for consumable goods, and areas outside those places to leave a vehicle. Retail car parks will remain in some form or other until the system collapses entirely, and my children's children are left to fight over the remaining resources in the last inhabitable spots on Planet Earth. With a bit of luck they will reorganise humanity with new priorities, new dreams and new challenges, of which parking will not be one. No more sixty-year-olds fighting over disabled bays. No rush hour arguments. No more boy-racers at night. Car parks will lie unattended, sprouting buddleia, as foxes rut and rats forage in the store interior. Eventually, forests will grow through the cracks, the tarmac crumbling deep into the earth, forming a grey layer around the planet, like a ring on a dirty bathtub, to be discovered by tentacled alien palaeontologists of the future when they dig deep into the rock. These cycloptic visitors to Earth might wonder what catastrophe befell the organisms who dominated the planet for such a brief window of time, before they slither back to their intergalactic spaceship, only to find they've been blocked in by some bloody idiot who doesn't know how to park a flying saucer properly.

Bibliography

Eran Ben-Joseph, *Rethinking a Lot: The Design and Culture of Parking*, The MIT Press, 2012

Kevin Beresford, *Parking Mad: Car Parks from Heaven (or Hell)*, Automobile Association, 2006

Tim Cresswell, *On The Move*, Routledge, 2006

T.S. Eliot, *Collected Poems 1909–1962*, Faber & Faber, 1963

Daniil Kharms, *Incidences*, Serpent's Tail, 1993

Pamela Lu, *Ambient Parking Lot*, Kenning Editions, 2011

Kathryn A. Morrison and John Minnis, *Carscapes: The Motor Car, Architecture, and Landscape in England*, Yale University Press, 2012

Phil Smith, *Mythogeography: A Guide to Walking Sideways*, Triarchy Press, 2012

Heathcote Williams, *Autogeddon*, Jonathan Cape, 1991

William Carlos Williams, *Selected Poems*, Penguin Modern Classics, 2000

Acknowledgements

Special thanks to:

Influx Press for their continued support of my writing.

Daniel Maudlin for Drake's Leat.

Martin Fuller for the filming. Jeff Pitcher for the photography. Simon Charterton and John Pope for the car park jazz odyssey. Mandy Curtis, Naomi Robinson & the Hastings Storytelling Festival.

The 4th World Congress of Psychogeography.

Weird Shit and Sheared Wit.

Maxi Bianco, Maxim Griffin, Mark Williamson, Michael Hambridge, Phil Wood, Phil Smith, Jane Campbell, Hester Campbell, Hamish Campbell, Chris Blumer, John Lavin, Nick Laight, Juliette Harris.

The cover crew: Venus and Isis Rees, Kirsty Otos, Dolly Otos, Teddy Otos, Kate Hockenhull, Katie & Vince Ray, Scarlett and Louie Musson, Ditte and Dave Cowan, Elaine Cass & Deeva, George and Sue Allison, Anna Mitchell, Andy Tompkins, Emma & Jim Welch, Daisy and Stamford Welch, Kate Hodges, Michelle Taylor-Knight, Sam Taylor-Knight, Sidney Garnett, Sam Kamara, Rachel Morgan, Liam Papuha and Matt Frost.

About the author

Gareth E. Rees is author of occult Hastings memoir *The Stone Tide* (Influx Press, 2018), and acclaimed psychogeographic work *Marshland* (Influx Press, 2013). He has written weird fiction and horror tales for titles including *This Dreaming Isle*, *The Shadow Booth: Vol. 2*, *Unthology 10* and *The Lonely Crowd*. He is the founder of the website Unofficial Britain (www.unofficialbritain.com), lead singer in garage punk band, The Dirty Contacts, and guitarist in psychedelic noise duo, Black Arches.

@hackneymarshman
@BritUnofficial

INFLUX
PRESS

Influx Press is an independent publisher based in London, committed to publishing innovative and challenging literature from across the UK and beyond. Formed in 2012, we have published titles ranging from award-nominated fiction debuts and site-specific anthologies to squatting memoirs and radical poetry.

www.influxpress.com
@Influxpress

THE STONE TIDE:
ADVENTURES AT THE END OF THE WORLD
Gareth E. Rees

Simultaneously quotidian and grotesque, *The Stone Tide* is the funniest, most readable, most intelligently self-searching book I've read in years.
— M John Harrison, author of *Light*

'The problems started the day we moved to Hastings…'

When Gareth E. Rees moves to a dilapidated Victorian house in Hastings he begins to piece together an occult puzzle connecting Aleister Crowley, John Logie Baird and the Piltdown Man hoaxer. As freak storms and tidal surges ravage the coast, Rees is beset by memories of his best friend's tragic death in St Andrews twenty years earlier. Convinced that apocalypse approaches and his past is out to get him, Rees embarks on a journey away from his family, deep into history and to the very edge of the imagination. Tormented by possessed seagulls, mutant eels and unresolved guilt, how much of reality can he trust?

The Stone Tide is a novel about grief, loss, history and the imagination. It is about how people make the place and the place makes the person. Above all it is about the stories we tell to make sense of the world.

ISBN: 9781910312070

MARSHLAND:
DREAMS AND NIGHTMARES ON
THE EDGE OF LONDON
Gareth E. Rees

'Whatever it is, New Weird, Cryptozoology, Psychogeography or Deep Map, *Marshland* is simply essential reading.'
— *Caught by the River*

'*Marshland* is essential reading – a psychedelic trip into London's secret wilderness.'
— John Rogers, author of *This Other London*

'*I had become a bit part in the dengue-fevered fantasy of a sick city.*'

Cocker spaniel by his side, Gareth E. Rees wanders the marshes of Hackney, Leyton and Walthamstow, avoiding his family and the pressures of life. He discovers a lost world of Victorian filter plants, ancient grazing lands, dead toy factories and tidal rivers on the edgelands of a rapidly changing city. Ghosts are his friends.

As strange tales of bears, crocodiles, magic narrowboats and apocalyptic tribes begin to manifest themselves, Rees embarks on a psychedelic journey across time and into the dark heart of London.

Marshland is a deep map of the east London marshes, a blend of local history, folklore and weird fiction, where nothing is quite as it seems.

ISBN: 9780957169395

BUILT ON SAND
Paul Scraton

'With a psychogeographer's sensibility and a deep connection to history, Paul Scraton's Built on Sand offers us a tender, fresh, and moving portrait of Berlin.'
— Saskia Vogel, author of *Submission*

'Sublime… Scraton has taken the broken memories of a city, refashioning them into a novel that's skewed and wondrous.'
— Irenosen Okojie, author of *Speak Gigantular*

Berlin: long-celebrated as a city of artists and outcasts, but also a city of teachers and construction workers. A place of tourists and refugees, and the m emories of those exiled and expelled. A city named after marshland; if you dig a hole, you'll soon hit sand.

Built on Sand centres on the personal geographies of place, and how memory and history live on in the individual and collective imagination. Stories of landscapes and a city both real and imagined; stories of exile and trauma, mythology and folklore; of how the past shapes and distorts our understanding of the present in an age of individualism, gentrification and the rising threat of nativism and far-right populism.

This novel offers a portrait of a city three decades on from the fall of the Berlin Wall, and the legacy of that history in a city that was once divided but remains fractured and fragmented.

ISBN: 9781910312339

HOW THE LIGHT GETS IN
Clare Fisher

'Cements her position as an innovative literary talent.'
— *New Statesman*

'Fisher's tales are funny and moving, and you'll treasure them all.'
— *Stylist*

'If fiction was a language, Clare Fisher would be one of its native speakers: a writer whose whole response to the world is brilliantly story-shaped.'
— Francis Spufford, author of *Golden Hill*

How The Light Gets In is the first collection from award winning short story writer and novelist, Clare Fisher. A book of very short stories that explores the spaces between light and dark and how we find our way from one to the other.

From buffering Skype chats and the truth about beards, to fried chicken shops and the things smartphones make you less likely to do when alone in a public place, Fisher paints a complex, funny and moving portrait of contemporary British life.

ISBN: 9781910312124

ATTRIB. AND OTHER STORIES
Eley Williams

WINNER OF THE JAMES TAIT BLACK PRIZE 2018

WINNER OF THE REPUBLIC OF CONSCIOUSNESS PRIZE 2018

'She is a writer for whom one struggles to find comparison, because she has arrived in a class of her own.'
— Sarah Perry, author of *Melmoth*

'It's just the real inexplicable gorgeous brilliant thing this book. I love it in a way I usually reserve for people.'
— Max Porter, author of *Lanny*

Attrib. and Other Stories celebrates the tricksiness of language just as it confronts its limits. Correspondingly, the stories are littered with the physical ephemera of language: dictionaries, dog-eared pages, bookmarks and old coffee stains on older books. This is writing that centres on the weird, tender intricacies of the everyday where characters vie to 'own' their words, tell tall tales and attempt to define their worlds.

With affectionate, irreverent and playful prose, the inability to communicate exactly what we mean dominates this bold debut collection from one of Britain's most original new writers.

ISBN: 9781910312162

SIGNAL FAILURE:
LONDON TO BIRMINGHAM, HS2 ON FOOT
Tom Jeffreys

'Through it all, Jeffreys's writing is intelligent, engaging and engaged, and deeply and disarmingly human.'
— *New Statesman*

'Tom Jeffreys is a worthy member of J.B.Priestley's good companions, and *Signal Failure* an engaging and affectionate update on that earlier writer s seminal English Journey.'
— Ken Worpole, author of *The New English Landscape*

One November morning, Tom Jeffreys set off from Euston Station with a gnarled old walking stick in his hand and an overloaded rucksack. His aim was to walk the 119 miles from London to Birmingham along the proposed route of HS2. Needless to say, he failed.

Over the course of ten days of walking, Jeffreys meets conservationists and museum directors, fiery farmers and suicidal retirees. From a rapidly changing London, through interminable suburbia, and out into the English countryside, Jeffreys goes wild camping in Perivale, flees murderous horses in Oxfordshire, and gets lost in a landfill site in Buckinghamshire. *Signal Failure* weaves together poetry and politics, history, philosophy and personal observation to form an extended exploration of people and place, nature, society, and the future.

ISBN: 9781910312148

BINDLESTIFF
Wayne Holloway

'A devastating vision of what America is becoming, wrapped up in a compelling and compassionate fable of what it is today.'
— Krishnan Guru-Murthy

'Holloway's latest work is bold, fresh, and an exciting contribution to Influx Press' enviable repertoire.'
— *The London Magazine*

2036. In a ramshackle, backwater United States, Marine Corp vet Frank Dubois journeys from L.A. to Detroit, seeking redemption for a life lived off the rails, in a country derailed from its own manifest destiny.

In present day Hollywood, a wannabe British film director hustles to get his movie 'Bindlestiff' off the ground starring 'Frank', a black Charlie Chaplin figure cast adrift in post-federal America.

Weaving together prose and screenplay *Bindlestiff* explores the power and responsibility of storytelling, revealing what lies behind the voices we read and the characters we see on screen. We open with a simple image of a man mending a hole in his shoe using a cut off piece of rubber and a tube of glue. From there the story explodes into a broiling satire on race, identity, family, friendship, war, peace, sex, drugs but precious little rock and roll.

ISBN: 9781910312292